Making Gourd Dolls & Spirit Figures

Ginger Summit & Jim Widess

Ginger Summit created all projects except the "Moose" in chapter 14, created by Jennifer Norpchen, and the wood-burned "Rodent"' in chapter 14, created by Tito Medina. The dolls were created by various gourd artists (*see* Index of Contributors). The three-part twining technique in chapter 7 was contributed by Cookie Cala.

Caution
Carving tools are sharp and dangerous. Wood-burning tools are extremely hot. Injury can result from the misuse or careless use of chisels, knives, drills, and saws. Sharp tools cause fewer accidents than dull tools. Use common sense, please. The dust resulting from carving gourds contains silica, mold particles, and who knows what else. Eye, nose, mouth, ear, and skin protection should be worn to prevent allergic or toxic reactions. The instructions and tops in this book are the synthesis of our experiences as well as those shared with us by more than a hundred gourd artists across the United States, Canada, and Europe. Your experiences may differ, but we hope they will be fulfilling and inspiring. Please direct any questions about gourd crafting to us at our email address: jimandginger@caning.com. Please write "Gourd Dolls" in the subject line.

Published by Echo Point Books & Media
Brattleboro, Vermont
www.EchoPointBooks.com

All rights reserved.
Neither this work nor any portions thereof may be reproduced, stored in a retrieval system, or transmitted in any capacity without written permission from the publisher.

Copyright © 2007, 2016 by Jim Widess and Ginger Summit

Making Gourd Dolls and Spirit Figures
ISBN: 978-1-63561-801-3 (paperback)

Interior design by Judy Morgan
Text by Ginger Summit
Photos by Jim Widess unless otherwise noted

Cover design by Adrienne Núñex

Contents

Introduction — 7
The Spirit in the Gourd — 7
What Is a Doll? — 10
History of Dolls — 16

CHAPTER ONE
Simple Whole Gourds — 24
Painted Whole Gourds — 26
Wood-Burned Whole Gourds — 33

CHAPTER TWO
Molded Gourds — 36
Naturally Collapsed Gourds — 36
Gourds Shaped While Growing — 38

CHAPTER THREE
Adding Limbs — 41
Stump Dolls — 42
Adding Arms & Legs — 45
Dolls with Articulated Joints — 59
Dolls with Articulated Complex Joints — 62
Marionettes — 64

CHAPTER FOUR
Dolls with Gourd Heads — 66
Wire-Armature Dolls — 66
Dolls with Cloth Bodies — 70

CHAPTER FIVE
Addition of Clay Parts — 75
Using Clay in Molds — 76
Sculpting Clay Faces — 80
Using Clay for Limbs & Other Shapes — 86

CHAPTER SIX
Stacked Dolls — 90
Combining Gourds — 90
Kokeshi Dolls, Kachinas & Other Dolls — 91

CHAPTER SEVEN
Fiber Arts & Beading — 108
Wrapping, Netting & Weaving — 108
Beadwork — 113

CHAPTER EIGHT
Cut & Carved Gourd Dolls — 118
Using Cut Shells — 119
Carving — 121

CHAPTER NINE
Dolls with Hidden Treasures & Nesting Dolls — 135
Creating Cavities — 135
Nesting — 142
Decorative Techniques — 145

CHAPTER TEN
Weighted Dolls — 149
Keeping Dolls Upright — 149
Daruma Dolls, African Initiation Dolls & Other Dolls — 150

CHAPTER ELEVEN
Instruments — 154
Sacred Images — 154
Hunter's Harp, Rattles & Other Instruments — 155

CHAPTER TWELVE
Puppets — 159
Stick Puppets — 160
Pop-Up Puppets — 162
Topsy-Turvy Puppets — 164
Finger Puppets — 166
Hand Puppets — 168
Puzzle Dolls & Mr. Gourd Head — 168

CHAPTER THIRTEEN
Jewelry & Ornaments — 171
Wearable Art — 171
Decorations for the Home — 176

CHAPTER FOURTEEN
Animals — 178

CHAPTER FIFTEEN
Gallery — 187

Index of Artists and Artworks — 218
General Index — 221

Gourd Doll & Spirit Figure Projects

PROJECT 1
Stump Doll — 43

PROJECT 2
Nisse — 46

PROJECT 3
Kitchen Witch — 57

PROJECT 4
Doll with Articulated Joints — 60

PROJECT 5
Dancing Dan — 63

PROJECT 6
Jesters — 68

PROJECT 7
Kokeshi Doll — 92

PROJECT 8
Stacked Dolls: Mother & Children — 97

PROJECT 9
Zulu Beaded Doll, Using Fabric — 114

PROJECT 10
Beaded Bottle Gourd, Using Fabric 115

PROJECT 11
Beaded Gourd, Using Tar 117

PROJECT 12
Spirit of Spring 123

PROJECT 13
Spirit of Summer 125

PROJECT 14
Autumn Spirit in the Tree 127

PROJECT 15
Spirit of Winter 130

PROJECT 16
Green Man 132

PROJECT 17
Mother Goose 141

PROJECT 18
Matryoshka Set 143

PROJECT 19
Weighted Daruma Doll 151

PROJECT 20
African Weighted Doll 153

PROJECT 21
Stick Puppets: Fairy Godmother 161

PROJECT 22
Pop-Up Puppets: Daybreak 163

PROJECT 23
Topsy-Turvy Puppets: Night & Day 165

PROJECT 24
Finger Puppets: The Three Little Pigs & Little Red Riding Hood 167

PROJECT 25
Puzzle Dolls: Humpty-Dumpty 169

PROJECT 26
Mr. Gourd Head 170

PROJECT 27
Moose 180

PROJECT 28
Rodent 185

Acknowledgments

We would like to thank the many artists who contributed artwork, comments, and techniques to this book. They were very generous with their encouragement. In particular, we would like to thank Diane Piccola for suggesting and advocating a book on the topic of gourd dolls and having the confidence in our being able to bring it to fruition. We also want to acknowledge Sterling Publishing's commitment to books on gourds, which are a major asset to the gourd-crafting world.

Many thanks to my patient husband Roger, who through the years has so graciously shared our life and home with gourds.
—Ginger Summit

And warm thanks to my wife Sher and our son Andy for your patience and love through these book projects.
—Jim Widess

Introduction

THE SPIRIT IN THE GOURD

Just as newly hatched birds and newborn mammals imprint from their mothers, the first visual image a human infant is predisposed to recognize is that of his or her mother. Recognizing familiar forms or configurations is so innate that we are inclined to see faces in almost anything when we first wake up or if we feel bleary-eyed. We look up at the clouds and make out recognizable shapes. We see the "man in the moon." Coupled with imagination, this natural instinct is the provenance of many artistic aspirations.

A pile of gourds speaks to this face-recognition and face-shaping ability as well as our imagination—if not by way of the particular shape of the gourd, then through the various subtle patterns and texture the moldy skin has left on the gourd's surface. The combination of shape and pattern virtually calls out to whomever is listening: "Take me!" "Look at me." "I'm a kitty-cat, I'm a swan." "Do you see my shape? I'm a spirit doll just waiting to be revealed in your hands."

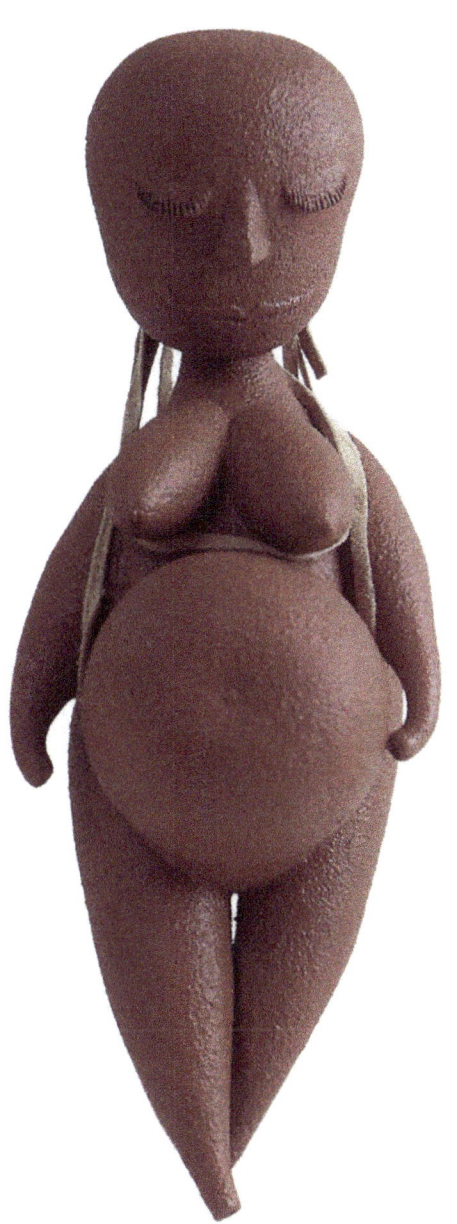

Goddess Doll,
Valerie Martinell

INTRODUCTION

Little gourd dolls, Andy Widess (son of co-author Jim Widess). Andy made these dolls when he was a toddler. He would play with the gourds before he ever drew facial features on them. Sometimes they would be people; other times they'd be little Volkswagens driving on the imaginary streets in the carpet.

Old Boyfriend Doll, Jennifer Brunswig. When angry with her old boyfriend, Jennifer could whip this doll, shaped like a punching bag, with a piece of basket reed.

Removing Mold

Before you can begin making your doll, you'll have to remove the moldy skin from your newly acquired collection of gourds. Mold is pernicious. You do not want to breathe in any mold spores, and it's not really a good idea for your skin to come into contact with mold either. *It's best to wear rubber gloves and a dust mask when you're handling the moldy gourds. If you tend to be allergic, you might consider wearing a more heavy-duty respirator.* The benefits of mold on gourds are that the mold separates the outer waterproof skin from the gourd so that you have a wonderful, woody surface upon which to draw, paint, wood-burn, or add clay, as well as the wonderful patterns the mold leaves on the gourd to inspire your imagination.

GOURD TIP

Here's the quickest way we've found to loosen the mold from the gourd without expending a lot of elbow grease. Gather your moldy gourds and put them into a black plastic garbage bag. Add a half-gallon of water, tightly seal the bag, and put the bag in the hot sun for a couple of hours. The humidity that builds up in the bag will loosen the mold and make it much easier to scrub off.

Three moldy, dirty gourds fresh from the farm. When first introduced to gourds, many artists look at these filthy fruits and just assume they are ruined and ready for the compost heap. Don't be fooled. Underneath the layer of black mold is a universe waiting to be explored.

Immerse the gourd in a bucket of warm soapy water. Let the moisture penetrate the outer layer, and then use a stainless-steel pot scrubber to take off the moldy skin. We've found that the stainless-steel scrubber works much better than the copper or plastic scrubbers. Steel wool is too fine. It clogs up quickly with the bits of skin.

The gourds are now clean and already conferring with each other as to what they would like to become.

Gourd Vision

When artist Leah Comerford begins working on a gourd, she rarely has a plan. She studies the gourd's markings until an image appears. "If nothing jumps out at me right away, I start looking for eyes," she says.

Her creativity and vision, of course, are personal and unique. Her technique, however, can be shared by anyone. Yet the resulting images will be different, as each artist sees the world through his or her own eyes and experiences.

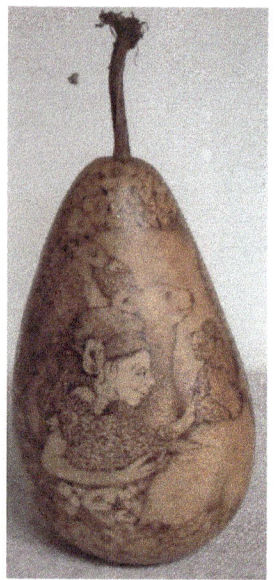

Here is Leah's vision after completing her pyrography (heat engraving or wood-burning). Photo by Jack Comerford.

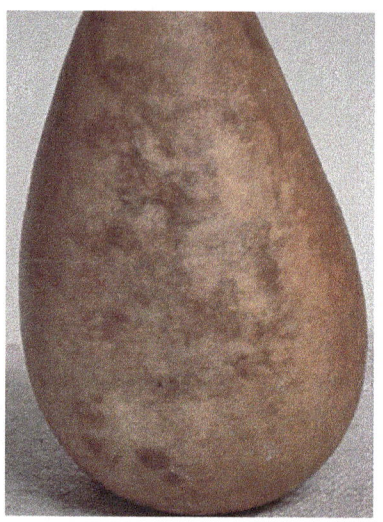

Washed and cleaned gourd, showing the splotchy mold patterns that occur naturally with field-dried gourds. Photo by Jack Comerford.

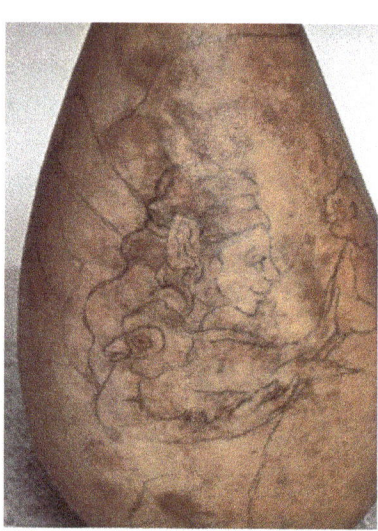

Leah pencils in the features as she sees them. She alters the nose and mouth slightly to enhance her vision of what she sees. Photo by Jack Comerford.

WHAT IS A DOLL?

When we think of the word *doll*, most of us picture a child's plaything or toy. But judging from the historical evidence, that concept is actually a relatively new one for articles made to resemble people.

Objects depicting humans are among the oldest forms of art known in the world. Scratches on bones and smooth stones found in excavations in Europe and Mesopotamia dating from the Paleolithic and Mesolithic periods provide evidence that from very earliest times, people were making human images. There has been a great deal of speculation as to the specific purpose of these objects. From the sheer number of small female figurines found in Anatolia (present-day Turkey) and parts of Europe, it's clear that goddess figures played an important role in the religions or traditional rites as long ago as 20,000 B.C.

One of the earliest goddess figures is the *Venus of Willendorf*, carved approximately 25,000 years ago. It was discovered at a Paleolithic site near Willendorf, Austria, and is thought to be an idealization of the female figure. Just over 4½ inches in height, this tiny figure has a large stomach and very pronounced breasts. The people who created this statuette/figurine were hunter-gatherers living in a harsh environment, so they probably regarded such characteristics of fatness and fertility to be highly desirable.

Other types of human figures have been found on all continents and in every known culture. Only those made of extremely durable substances such as bone, stone, and fired clay have survived, although based on present-day examples, it can be assumed that similar images were constructed of any materials available to the local people.

Venus of Willendorf, *Lillian Hopkins.* This small gourd figure is approximately the same size and shape as the well-known carving dating from some 25,000 years ago, now housed in the Naturhistorisches Museum in Vienna. Simple wood burning and added air-drying clay suggests the voluptuousness of this most famous of the ancient goddess figures.

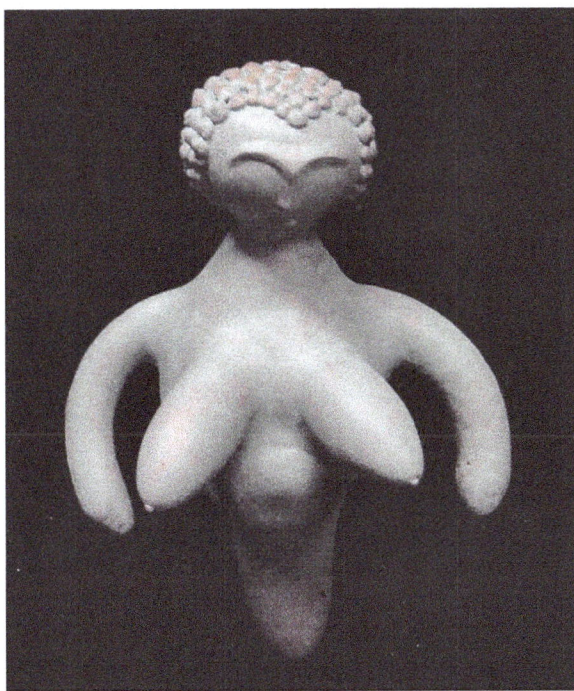

Gourd Goddess, *Larry McClelland*

Goddess, *Carolyn Potter*. The artist combined two gourds with a ceramic-doll head, copper *milagros* (small amulets commemorating a miracle, from the Hispanic tradition), and wire for hair. The doll was rubbed with tar to antique the body and to attach the *milagros*.

Archaeologists and anthropologists who have collected these very old objects generally agree that they were not intended as playthings but were sacred objects used by the priestly members of the community. In general, these figures (effigies) were not meant to represent specific people but were prototypes of humans and humanlike spirits, both male and female. Their primary function was as a vehicle for communicating with the spirit world in rituals pertaining to initiation, fertility, marriage, and burial.

Mina Perdida Effigy

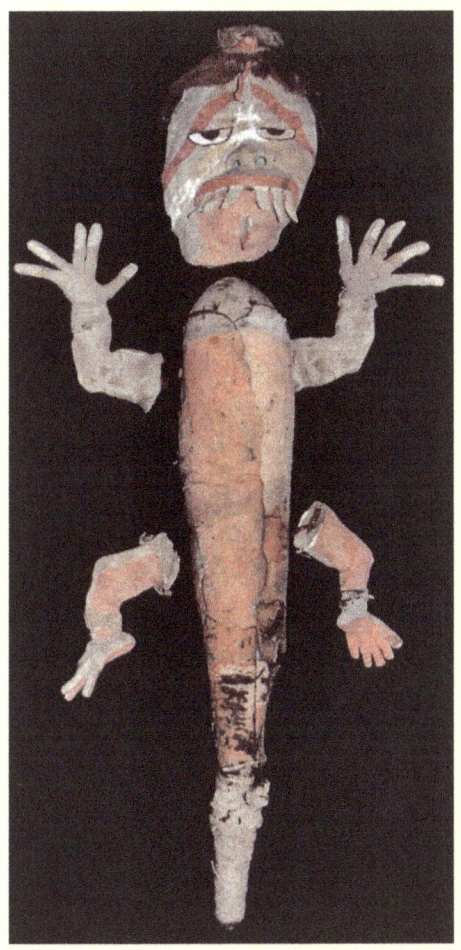

Mina Perdida effigy. Photo courtesy of Richard L. Burger.

With the fangs of the ferocious black cayman and the facial markings of the aplomado falcon, this extraordinary effigy, one of the oldest anthropomorphic gourd figures known, is more than 3,000 years old. Radiocarbon dating was done by analyzing a seed that was still attached to the interior of the 22-inch (55-cm) bottle-gourd body of the effigy. A frequently depicted icon of this period, the figure was discovered at a site called Mina Perdida (Lost Mine) in Peru.

Its distinctive topknot hairstyle was created with great care. Fine cordage connects the articulated arms and legs to the gourd body. The lower part of the bottle gourd, wrapped with cordage, was probably used as a handle to hold the figure with its outstretched hands high in the air. This effigy was found wrapped in a brown-and-white cotton cloth. Clothing of the period was usually wrapped in the same way.

Confronting this supernatural effigy, with its enormous mouth and gigantic crocodile-like fangs, is awe-inspiring. The red-painted body communicates energy and awareness. The facial markings of the falcon and Andean condor suggest the power of flight high above the earth.

"Imagine a torchlight ceremony on the top of Mina Perdida, with winds blowing off the ocean and stars carpeting the sky. Suddenly a terrifying, strange, yet almost human supernatural being, cloaked in a cotton garment, leaps into view, its limbs swaying and hair blowing. Enormous fangs jut from its mouth, its huge hands are raised and spread wide, and a strange disembodied voice issues from its fanged and bloody mouth telling of an unseen world and a mythical time, both of which suddenly seem very real indeed."

—Richard L. Burger and
Lucy Salazar-Burger,
"A sacred effigy from Mina Perdida."
RES 33, Spring 1998, Peabody
Museum of Archaeology and
Ethnology, Cambridge,
Massachusetts.

Doll from Brazil, made from tree gourds, used in a young woman's initiation into puberty.

The etymology of the word *doll* is not certain. Some authors suggest that it came from the Greek name Dorothea, which means "a gift expressing honor" or "to enter a temple to offer a gift or sacrifice." Another possible source is from the Greek word *eidolon*, or "idol," which would demonstrate the religious context. Later, the Latin term *pupa*, French *poupée*, and German *puppe*, meaning "little girl," came into use, suggesting a completely different function for these human figures.

There is a fundamental distinction between the concepts "figure" or "figurine," "doll," and "puppet." Historically, *figures* or *figurines* were assumed to have a spiritual meaning, because they were used in religious rites or ceremonies to represent an intermediary between the physical and nonphysical worlds. Because of this function, only diviners, shamans, healers, or others who held a position of power in the society handled them. In contrast, *dolls* may or may not have specific meanings imbedded in them, and they are intended for personal use. An almost universal function of the doll has been as a gift to young girls or women to care for as a token of coming of age or desire for children. While dolls are common even today in Africa in this role, they were also used traditionally in Italy as part of a bride's dowry, where the bride was encouraged to bathe and feed the doll in preparation for raising her own family. In France, newlyweds often took dolls to bed in hopes of conception. Dolls became incorporated into personal activities and role-playing and populated an imaginary world of their owners.

Puppets, were intended to educate and used to create an imaginary world for an audience. When applied to education, they were a means of transmitting the values and social mores of the culture or tribe. They were also used as a vehicle for the spirits to communicate messages to groups of people. Puppets traditionally had a more public role in performances, as opposed to the personal, more intimate function of the doll.

Even when dolls were given to children as playthings, they were intended primarily as a way to educate children about specific roles in society. For example, in Japan, the intricacies of ceremonies were acted out through dolls. In most cultures, dolls are considered to be the domain of girls or young women. Their function is to provide a means of learning future roles, especially those pertaining to caring for and nurturing another being. Today, dolls, as playthings, are available for both boys and girls to incorporate into a wide variety of role-playing scenarios. Through this interaction, children develop a sense of their own identities and the complex interplay of responsibilities within the community.

In this book, we have accepted the broadest possible definition of dolls so as to include a wide variety of examples. Many are intended only for display and introspection, while others are definitely created for playful interaction.

The projects in this book are designed to introduce the broadest range of creative options for the artist, from basic construction methods to embellishment techniques. Many show how to make dolls that are common to a specific cultural tradition. While respecting the traditions and heritage surrounding these figures, we encourage you to use the construction and decorative techniques herein for other figures as well.

Folk art Mexican gourd puppet. Collection of Dyan Mai Peterson. Photo by Tim Barnwell, Asheville, North Carolina.

HISTORY OF DOLLS

Dolls, or human figures, were made long before recorded history, throughout the world. From their remains, it is nearly impossible to exactly identify their purpose or the role they played. Because of the large number found, however, anthropologists and historians are quite certain that these effigies had numerous functions. The objects that could survive thousands of years were made of durable materials such as stone, bone, and ceramic that could withstand harsh circumstances. Probably many other human types of objects were made of materials that decay, are eaten by insects or rodents, or otherwise do not last long periods of time.

Most human figures that have been found are associated with burial sites in locations as far apart as Egypt, Mesopotamia, South America, North America, Asia, and Australia. The purposes of these figures can only be surmised, but it's frequently assumed that they were part of religious or ceremonial rites.

Figures found in abundance in Anatolia are thought to represent the feminine spirit or earth goddess. Those found in graves around the world are believed to represent either ancestors or tomb servants meant to perform tasks for the dead in the next life.

Many of the earliest figures have the simplest of markings, usually eyes or perhaps suggestions of breasts and genitals or other markings deemed important to the particular society, such as a shaped head or scarification. Yet dolls made of carved wood with beaded hair and paint dating as far back as 3,000 B.C. have been found in graves in such disparate places as Egypt, Mayan sites in Mexico, and China.

Religion, nature, and human interaction are the three basic forces that inspire creative imagination, both in ceremonies and in artistic expression, regardless of the century, location, or society. This explains the consistency we find in the use of human figures in ceremonies in different societies throughout the world. They were often used as an intermediary between the known and unknown worlds in an attempt to influence forces beyond human control. Depending on the specific demands of the religions, the figures may have been used as a substitute for human sacrifice or to represent the gods or spirits that came to visit tribes or homes. In all situations, however, the depictions were an expression of the power and mystery of divine forces, and they were often the exclusive property

Medicine gourd doll from Tanzania. Collection of Dyan Mai Peterson. Photo by Tim Barnwell, Asheville, North Carolina.

HISTORY OF DOLLS 17

Above, Hemba/Luba pipe from the Democratic Republic of Congo. The central figure and two additional heads are mounted on a gourd. Collection of Ginger Summit.

Left, Indonesian gourd scarecrow. Collection of Dyan Mai Peterson. Photo by Tim Barnwell, Asheville, North Carolina.

of the shaman or healer. Fetishes were frequently set up in special shrines, where they were fed and cared for with great respect. Remnants of these practices continue in many cultures throughout the world to this day, and many of the images represented in this book are expressions of these rituals.

Although dolls were frequently used as fetishes or talismans in spiritual activities, it is quite likely that they were often used in play among the children as well. Yet there is no archaeological evidence to support this. Perhaps the objects made for ceremonies were created out of more durable materials, while those given to children for play were created out of materials that would decay or decompose. This is supported by the evidence of many dolls, made for children today in far-flung parts of the world, made of wood, seeds, corncobs, bundles of cloth or straw, and especially squashes, yams, and gourds. Even when dolls are used in play, however, the children are mimicking the child-rearing patterns of their cultures, learning valuable lessons of nurturing and care.

Europe

While many Western people may view the ritual figures found in other cultures as strange or as an oddity, a close look at Western European traditions throughout history will reveal a similar use of human images. Greek and Roman statuary indicates a fascination with and excellence in creating representations of the human figure. Similar smaller objects have been found in the tombs of children and at shrines of specific gods and goddesses. In pagan cultures throughout Europe, the tradition of spirits, both harmful and beneficial, was an important part of folklore. These images can be seen today in the hobgoblins of Norway and Sweden and in the gnomes, gremlins, and sprites that are popular in Germanic cultures and in their dolls and figures.

Within the Christian tradition, churches and shrines are often elaborately decorated with images of saints and members of the Holy Family. Like icons in other cultures, these figures were never intended to be the subject of worship themselves, but rather a means to instruct and remind the faithful of lessons acquired in church. Occasionally the Holy Family is depicted in crèche scenes that may cross the line into playthings for children.

The first known dolls that were made commercially as playthings for children appeared in the fifteenth and sixteenth centuries in Germany. They were primarily adults dressed in the fashion of the day and were perhaps intended to represent images of people in court. The first childlike dolls did not appear until the 1800s, when a "baby" doll was introduced in Germany.

China

Human statuary has a long history in China, both as tomb figures to be buried with the dead to assist in the next life and as parts of shrines in the household. These representations could personify either departed ancestors or titular deities. They were not worshipped but rather were considered amulets or good-luck symbols. This custom continues to this day, with the images well cared for with presents and food, in hopes of securing good health and fortune.

In China and elsewhere around the world where it is important to preserve a woman's modesty, healers often have very anatomically correct figurines that a woman (or her servant) could use to describe an ailment without actually revealing her body. A related service of dolls was to act as a magical surrogate for the ill person, to be given the germs or evil spirits making the person sick. The likeness was then burned, both to heal the victim as well as to protect the other family members from sickness.

Africa

Most sub-Saharan African cultures have a long tradition of dolls representing many different concepts. Probably the most widespread, and certainly the most recognized and perhaps misunderstood, is the use of dolls as fertility spirit figures. The concept of fertility does not pertain just to the individual woman's ability to have children, although it certainly includes this. It also has to do with the fertility and abundance of nature. These cultures are entirely dependent on the balance of natural forces, the people, the animals, and the land. It is obvious to all that super-magical powers control this, and therefore special rites and ceremonies are invoked to ensure the continued health of the entire village world. Dolls are often given to girls during puberty rites as part of the instruction for their future role and

Hemba/Luba rattle from Democratic Republic of Congo. Collection of Ethnic Arts, Berkeley, California.

responsibility in the tribe. On emerging from seclusion, the girls wear these dolls to symbolize their changed status and the implicit readiness for childbearing.

Rather than belonging to individuals in the tribe, other dolls play a role in the shaman's rituals. The dolls may be decorated with powerful talismans, such as bones, nails, or ointments, with which to attract specific spirits. Sometimes small bottle gourds are used to hold powerful medicines. The fetish gourds themselves are decorated with beads or carving, and the stoppers are carved to represent either ancestors or the powers that aid the shaman.

If a child is missing in the forest or bush, a human image is often placed out there along with food to attract the forest spirit. As the spirit is distracted, the living child is able to escape and return home.

And finally, dolls are created as amulets to surround an infant, primarily to ward off evil spirits that may harm the child.

Nyamwezi doll from Tanzania. Collection of Dyan Mai Peterson. Photo by Tim Barnwell, Asheville, North Carolina.

South America

The Jivaras, in the Amazon basin, took the heads of enemies slain in battle to paralyze the spirit of their enemies so that they could not return to wreak havoc among the survivors or seek revenge among the spirits of the ancestors. When the custom of shrinking the actual heads declined, or if it was impossible to retrieve the head of a fallen enemy during battle, the warrior took a gourd and attached some of the dead man's hair to it with wax. This served to represent the victim's soul, which would no longer be able to bring harm to the living or the dead.

Beaded figure, Fernando Vargas

Spirit figure, Fernando Vargas

Amil Pedro

An authentic member of the Gila River Indian community, Amil Pedro grew up with gourds. His earliest memory is of helping his uncles and the elders make gourd dippers, canteens, and rattles. He has been working with gourds ever since, for more than fifty years.

When making a figure, he visualizes the completed project and works to that end. He has developed his own style and techniques, which usually work as he anticipates. While a medicine man's gourd is sacred, other gourds are a wonderful canvas for his own artwork. Currently, Amil is working on a series of figures, "Honoring the Clay Doll," which is his interpretation of the dolls made for the tourist trade in the 1890s. Through his gourds, he honors those who came before him.

Gourd figure made with beads and paint, Amil Pedro

Stylized gourd figure, Amil Pedro

Bill Colligen

Bill Colligen has always had artistic interests and talents. When he was a small boy in New Hampshire, he was called "Billy, the boy artist." He worked with many different materials, including stone, before he finally saw gourds being used for art in the nineties. Fascinated by the variety of shapes, he began working with them, and starting in 2000 devoted himself full time to his art.

Fetish pot, Bill Colligen. The artifacts of the prehistoric Casa Grandes people of northern New Mexico were the inspiration for this piece.

CHAPTER ONE
Simple Whole Gourds

Japan: Gourds have been used in Japan for centuries as containers and drinking vessels. Here, an imposing face was painted on a cleaned and polished gourd, used to guard the household against any evil spirits. Collection of Ginger Summit.

Because gourds come in such a wide variety of shapes and sizes, it is very easy to envision a human form residing in an existing gourd, needing very little manipulation to emerge. Often all that is required is some simple wood-burning, painting, or etching to define and enhance the human features. These forms can be further embellished with wrapped fabrics, feathers, leather, or other materials to enrich the spirit being represented.

Single gourds with minimal embellishments are frequently found as tourist items in countries where gourds are readily available and often used as household containers.

Turkey: Throughout the Mediterranean and Middle East, gourds have been used through the millennia as containers for oils, snuff, gunpowder, water, and household goods. These small bottle gourds were painted to resemble a man and woman wearing traditional Turkish garb. Collection of Ginger Summit.

Peru: These carved and wood-burned figures are depicted wearing traditional clothing and playing instruments much like those played in festivals throughout Peru. Collection of Ginger Summit.

PAINTED WHOLE GOURDS

Nancy Schlender

"The gourd speaks to me," Nancy Schlender says. "Even when I begin with a plan in mind, it always changes as the gourd dictates." She has always been in awe of the uniqueness and beauty of the colorful ornamental gourds. When she is embellishing, she feels the gourd doll tells her what it desires as it emerges and comes to life. "I do not permanently attach embellishments until we are both happy with them," she says.

French Chef, *Cass Iverson*. This saucy French chef was painted onto an elongated Indonesian bottle gourd. Clay feet were added to provide stability.

Inuit, *Nancy Schlender*

PAINTED WHOLE GOURDS **27**

Sundance, *Nancy Schlender*

African "Voodoo," *Sidney Embry*

Geri Gittings

When she saw a gourd for the first time, Geri Gittings exclaimed, "What's that?!" But that was the moment her gourd career was launched, and she hasn't looked back since, except to reflect on how she has never enjoyed anything as much as she enjoys working with gourds. "A gourd enables me to do a two-dimensional piece of art on something three-dimensional," she says. "Instead of working on a flat surface with oils, watercolors, or pastels, I can do all that and more. I can also carve and wood-burn, which opens up a whole new facet in the world of creating. I love working on gourds!"

Lady of the Lake, *Matt Barna. Photo by Matt Barna.*

Gourd Maiden, *Geri Gittings*

Deborah Easley

Her life in art began at the age of four, with dance. Since that time, Deborah Easely has explored drawing and painting, and pursued this interest while attending college at the California School of Professional Fabric Design.

Gourds have provided an entirely different medium to investigate another step in her artistic development. She says, when working with gourds, two things can happen: "From a mysterious space of creation, a feeling intuition of an image takes form, and I look for a gourd that fits the shape of that vision. Or, after looking at a gourd for years, I suddenly see it in a new way that leads to a new piece of art." For her, gourds symbolize "a return to wholeness in our fragmented world."

Her piece *La Llorona* is based upon the legend of *La Llorona* (the Weeping Woman). A ghostly figure, *La Llorona* is said to have wandered through the waterways of the Southwest wailing, "Where are my children?" For several weeks before starting this piece, Deborah felt a great deal of grief over the loss of so many young people around the world, whether from war, accidents, or disease. "I chose the theme of *La Llorona* as an experiment in productively processing my feelings," she explains.

Kachina, *Robert Rivera.*
Collection of Sher Elliott-Widess.

La Llorona, *Deborah Easley*

Serenity, *Marilyn Buhler*

Marilyn Buhler

Marilyn Buhler started growing her own gourds after a friend sent her seeds and told her she could grow anything in California. Since then, she has been hooked on gourd projects, "overwhelmed with the freedom of expression and possibilities," she explains. She always tries something new with each project, "to give it a sense of spirituality and a feeling of closeness to the earth."

Elizabeth Ritz-Frith

Raised in a family of artists, Elizabeth Ritz-Frith has been experimenting with different media all her life. She first encountered gourds in an online decorative painting group. One member wrote about her experience decorating gourds, and Elizabeth became hooked. "I often buy gourds from the Internet," she says. "I'm afraid if I ever went to a gourd farm I'd want them all."

She starts from a basic idea and then selects a gourd. "But often a gourd sends its own message," she says, "and you have to go with it. The gourd is a natural thing from the earth and therefore takes 'natural' embellishments well. I feel that the gourd is beautiful, so why cover it up? Working with gourds makes me feel more connected to the earth. There is something about them that says, 'Don't make me look like something plastic.'"

Carol Papner

"I start with an image or design in my mind and look for a gourd that will fit what I want to do," says Carol Papner. "I go through piles of gourds. I enjoy digging through them to find the perfect ones for what I want to create. I never really believed artists who said a piece speaks to them, but I have now become a believer."

For her kachina figures, Carol painted mini-gourds with acrylics and embellished them with clay and feathers and beads.

PAINTED WHOLE GOURDS **31**

Left, Pueblo Sun Gourd Doll, *Elizabeth Ritz-Frith.* This is a simple painted doll. The hole where the sun mask fits was already in the gourd, so all that was needed was a small piece of dowel to attach it. This figure is painted on a portion of a snake gourd. The mask is similar to a kachina dancer's mask. It was cut from a second gourd and shaped to fit over the face.

Mini Badger Kachina, *Carol Papner*

32 SIMPLE WHOLE GOURDS

Mini Eagle Kachina, *Carol Papner*

Maiden, *Kristi Dial*

WOOD-BURNED WHOLE GOURDS

Buddha, *Jo Cooley*. Wood-burning and dyes transformed this gourd into a Buddha. Carving away the external shell produced the contrasting pale face.

Rattle, *Jennifer Loe*

Janis Kobe

Although she has always been an artist, Janis Kobe felt a very direct connection to gourds. She attended a gourd workshop in northern California with a friend and has been working with gourds ever since. "When I look at a pile of gourds, one will 'whistle' to me and tell me what it wants to be," she says. "The gourd then becomes the inspiration." She maintains a great respect for all of nature, which to her is sacred. But her artistic muse is not limited to gourds—she will use any materials if they are right for the project at hand.

Mumso, *Janis Kobe*

Christi Tsai

Christi Tsai brings to her gourd art a background in ceramics, silk painting, and Chinese brush painting. "The gourd will normally give me a hint of what it wants to be," she says. "When I get an idea, I'll sketch it on a gourd or in my sketchbook. When I have time, I'll wood-burn it onto a gourd." Christi is particularly attracted to the gourd's unique shapes and pleased to be able to apply her past art experience to working with gourds. "And, of course, in my Chinese culture," she explains, "the whole gourd is a good-luck symbol."

Sleeping Angel, *Christi Tsai*

Let Me See, *Christi Tsai*

Love, *Christi Tsai*

Connie Mygatt

Having an interest in art since she was a small child, Connie Mygatt later pursued art in college, specializing in portraiture. She was attracted to working with gourds for many reasons, including the varied shapes they offered and the three-dimensional quality they could bring to her art. Many gourd shows and encounters with gourd artists convinced her that this was an important new direction in her art career. On her first visit to a gourd farm, Connie found that many of the different-shaped gourds spoke to her. Yet one stood out more than the others, a small bottle gourd, which she turned into a Native American wearing a blanket. With the success of that project ten years ago, she embarked on a career focusing on figures in gourd art. "I like to keep as true to the form as I can," she says. "I draw the face directly on the gourd and keep the designs simple, mostly petroglyph or geometric designs. I feel the soul of the gourd speaks through the face I create on the gourd."

The Wise One, *Connie Mygatt*

Old Bead Stringer, *Connie Mygatt*

CHAPTER TWO
Molded Gourds

Artist Pat Duncan used the Pickle Puss mold to create the head of this delightful doll.

While growing, gourds can be put into a mold or otherwise manipulated to change their shape until they are mature and dried. The Chinese are masters of this practice and create molds for gourds to produce extremely elaborate objects and vessels. In the United States, plastic molds made for vegetables have been fastened around very young gourds to create novelty faces. It is always a challenge to identify a gourd that will grow to just the right size and proportion to fit the mold when mature.

NATURALLY COLLAPSED GOURDS

After gourds have been harvested, occasionally some will shrink and become distorted because the outer shell was not fully mature when the vine died. While these shells are usually discarded, some artists are particularly motivated to discover the hidden faces within the folds.

Leigh Adams

Having been an artist all her life, Leigh Adams has worked with a wide variety of materials. She had known about gourds through anthropology classes, but it wasn't until she took a class in gourd crafting that all the pieces came together. At this time, gourds are a very important part of her life, not just as an artist. She uses them when she teaches in the classroom and most recently has followed the gourd trail to China.

Figure made from a naturally collapsed gourd, Leigh Adams

Flower Fairy, Leigh Adams. The Flower Fairy's hair is a dipper-gourd handle that was manipulated while growing by wrapping the handle around a rope. Photo by Leigh Adams.

GOURDS SHAPED WHILE GROWING

Several plastic molds are designed to shape vegetables as they are growing. They can easily be secured around a young gourd as well. The challenge is to identify a gourd that will mature to a suitable size and shape to fill out the mold proportionally.

The baby gourd is placed carefully into the mold a day or two after the flower has been pollinated successfully. The mold should be supported so that the weight of the gourd and mold does not tax the stem. Be sure to have the mold in the shade and not in direct sunlight or where water can get inside the mold. Leave the gourd in the mold until the gourd is fully mature with at least 6 inches (15 cm) of dried stem coming out of it. Some molds are designed to hold the entire gourd, whereas others (VegiForms' Pickle Puss, for example) are intended to be placed only on the end of a banana or snake gourd.

Mr. Ugly *(one of three faces), Pat Duncan.* Mr. Ugly *was grown in a glass fishbowl that stayed filled with water because there were no drain holes. After it broke out of its bowl, but the gourd just kept growing, with knobs. "When it was dry," says the artist, "my daughter and I found three faces."*

For this piece, artist Virginia Saunders removed the gourd from the Garden Elf mold before it was fully mature, so that the gourd continued to grow and the sharp features from the mold softened as the gourd grew in diameter.

GOURDS SHAPED WHILE GROWING 39

Baby on the Way, *Dyan Mai Peterson*. The gourd used for this figure was constrained by randomly tied cord while it was growing. The resulting lumpiness evoked Baby on the Way. Photo by Tim Barnwell, Asheville, North Carolina.

Here are two different results of the VegiForms Pickle Puss mold. The dolls were created by Pat Duncan

Chinese Molded Gourds

During the Cultural Revolution of the 1960s and 1970s, many Chinese cultural traditions were lost. But recently the Zhang family in northeastern China has rekindled the complex agronomy of molding gourds.

Molded-gourd Santa Claus. Designed and grown by Cairi Zhang and Gang Zhang, Gourd Island Gourd Society, Liaoning, China. Collection of Sher Elliott-Widess.

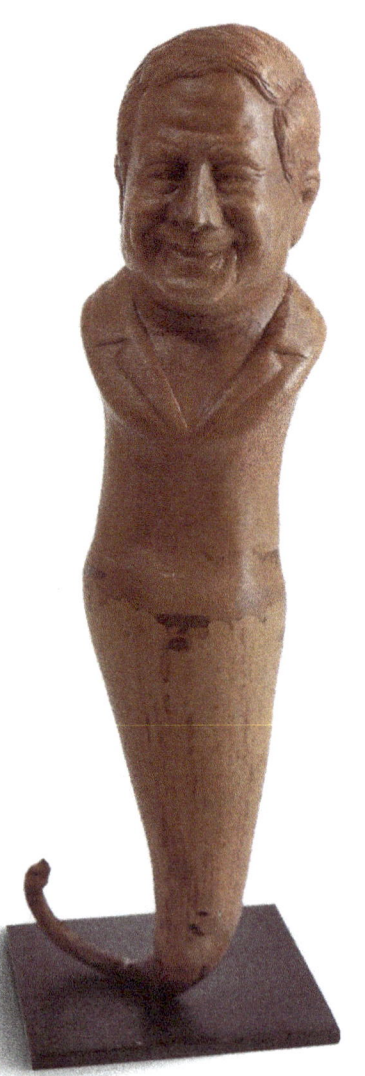

Gourd Jim. Figure made from a fully mature gourd taken from a plaster mold. A dyed finish has been added to the gourd. Designed and grown by Cairi Zhang and Gang Zhang, Gourd Island Gourd Society, Liaoning, China.

Chinese folk god of longevity, one of the eight immortals. Molded gourd designed by Cairi Zhang and Gang Zhang, Gourd Island Gourd Society, Liaoning, China.

CHAPTER THREE
Adding Limbs

Because of the rounded shape of the gourd, many artists envision a body that only needs limbs to fully realize the spirit within. Frequently only arms are added, leaving the rest of the gourd to be embellished and the imagination of the viewer to supply missing parts. The added limbs can be made of nearly any material at all, depending on the artist's preferences and vision. Parts of other gourds may be used, but just as often, limbs are constructed of twigs, carved wood, wire and other metals, clay, and cloth. Depending on how they are attached, these additions can be rigid or movable.

Pinocchio, *Ginger Summit*

STUMP DOLLS

Stump dolls have appeared in most cultures from very early times, but the origin is often incorrectly attributed to the early settlers in North America, who carved simple doll forms out of tree limbs and painted or carved minimal facial features. This very rudimentary stump-doll body shape typically had no joints or legs. Children or young women would drape this shape with cloth or leaves to create clothing.

Other figures also called "stump dolls" were made of cloth, vegetables, and gourds, and were found in Europe dating from the sixteenth century. Similar figures were found in Egyptian tombs, in many parts of Asia, and throughout Africa. Their common feature is that they have no legs and may or may not have arms.

The gourd lends itself to this type of doll quite naturally. A bottle gourd or short-handled dipper gourd needs only the addition of a head and any type of adornment or clothing that is typical of the culture.

Three Seminole dolls, Juanita Moreno. This artist has used gourds to replicate the traditional Seminole doll. The bright paints evoke the beautiful patchwork clothing for which the Seminoles are known.

Seminole dolls do not have limbs, making them an excellent example of the early stump dolls. The Seminoles are a blending of mainly Creek Indians from Georgia and Alabama who migrated to Florida in the 1700s. Living in the Everglades, they originally made dolls of palmetto palm fronds, cinching the fronds at the neck to create a head. This form was traditionally draped with a skirt and cape made of scraps from their distinctive pieced cotton, topped with a black hat. These simple dolls were typically made for tourists, and this practice continues today.

PROJECT 1

Stump Doll

For this project, simple arms are added along with the head. The arms are cut from a separate gourd and carved to conform to the shape of the body.

1. Select two small gourds, and drill a hole in the top of the body to accommodate the head.

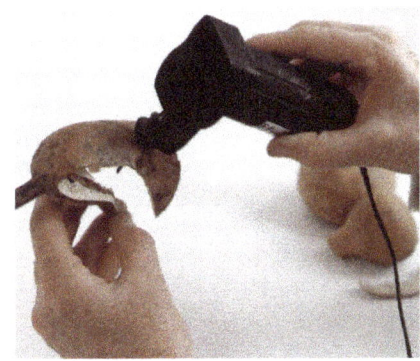

2. From a separate gourd scrap, cut two arms. The top of a bottle gourd was selected to best create a shoulder. Sand the edges, and use a leather awl to make small holes in the arms and body.
Continued on page 44.

This doll is embellished with a simple wig of black yarn, painted features, and a gathered cotton skirt.

44 ADDING LIMBS

3. Secure a small bead at the end of a length of florist wire, and draw it through the arm and body.

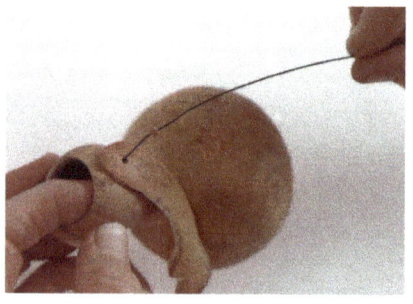

4. Attach a bead to the other end of the florist wire, and twist to tighten.

5. The gourd arms are attached to the body before the doll is dressed.

Robert Irwin

"When I create something from a gourd, I spend quite a bit of time just waiting for a spark of inspiration. I have no preconceived idea of what I am going to do. Even as I work, I don't hold tight to the concept—I let the gourd lead me. Each doll comes to life slowly. One gourd may say 'body,' and I have to hunt for a head. Or a gourd may say 'head,' and I search for a body. The process is very slow. After I have a head and a body, I have to find the right embellishments, some hair or some eyes, some key to finding the personality or spirit of the doll. I just keep going until I'm done, or until the doll is done with me. I feel a sacredness about art. I think a society could be judged by its art and by the way the society feels about art and artists."

This doll, created by Robert Irwin, is very similar to a "stump doll," in that it consists of a gourd body, with only the head and arms attached.

ADDING ARMS & LEGS

The next step in creating a more complete image of the human figure is to add both arms and legs. Artists have used many different kinds of materials to create limbs, such as wire, wood dowels, twigs, and clay. As the figures become more complex, more embellishments are added to evoke a specific identity for the figure.

Hobgoblins of Norway and Sweden

In many countries throughout Europe, wood-turned dolls have been made for centuries. They may consist of a single piece of wood turned on a lathe to create a head and body, or simple pegs and beads of a variety of shapes and sizes that are combined to create human or fantasy figures. Often these creations are painted with colors and patterns that reflect typical traditional clothing.

This style of figure is particularly popular in Scandinavia, where the *nisse* (Norway) and the *tomte* (Sweden) are a large part of folklore. These creatures are hobgoblins who live in the fields and woods, never harming the nearby humans. According to legend, the Norwegian hobgoblins live in the barn, watching over the family and animals, occasionally playing tricks but mostly keeping the household safe. They wear a bright-red cap to identify themselves to the birds of prey, which leave them in peace. The Norwegian and Swedish hobgoblins are brought to life by the wooden figures popular at Christmastime, the *Jule nisse* and *Jule tomte*. Although they are traditionally made with wooden shapes, the small bottle gourd can easily be transformed into these delightful creatures to enhance any holiday fantasy.

Gourd doll with attached arms, Gabrielle Hunter

PROJECT 2

Nisse

Because small bottle gourds resemble the bodies of the wood-turned dolls often found throughout Europe, it is quite simple to make these charming creatures with gourds instead of turned wood.

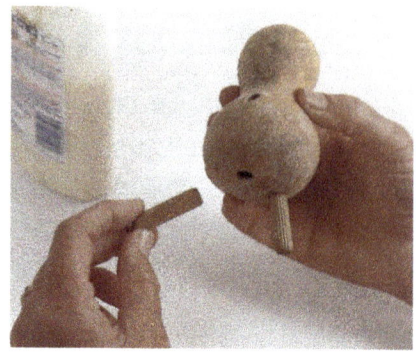

1. Drill holes in the base of a small bottle gourd to fit the small dowel legs.

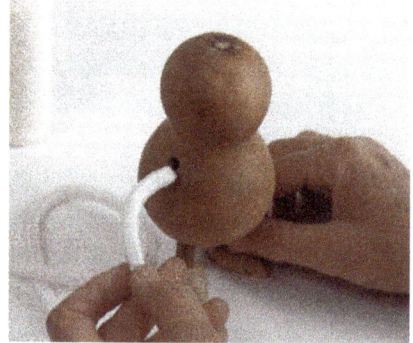

2. Drill holes in the upper body for the rope arms, and glue in place.

3. Once the glue is dry, embellish the figure to complement any season or decor. For example, a *Jule nisse* could be made for the Christmas season.

ADDING ARMS & LEGS

Holiday figures (leprechaun and witch), Ginger Summit

Troll, Ginger Summit

Aunt Mabel at Mardi Gras, *Gerri Bishop*

Gerri Bishop

Gerri Bishop became hooked on gourds after wood-burning one. She had been taking care of her husband, who was housebound by injuries, when a friend showed her the gourds she had been carving. She was excited by being able to express her artistic spirit and finds working with gourds extremely gratifying. While creating, she explains, "I enter a world of my own, where my mind can relax and play, while troubles melt away." She says she watches her silly creations grow into something that makes her smile inside and out. For her, gourds are "amazing in their usefulness and endless possibilities."

Susan Begin

Arts and crafts devotee Susan Begin discovered gourds while researching to provide focus for her work. She was intrigued that she found gourds used in nearly every culture, past and present, and was fascinated with them on her visits to Central America. When she picked them up, she says, "I had more ideas than I could remember, since they provided a surface that was suitable for drawing and painting, and could be carved, manipulated, and combined with a variety of mixed media. I have been passionate about gourds ever since. The gourd is a wonderful source of inspiration, ready to accept whatever technique or medium an artist may utilize."

Gourdling, *Susan Begin*. Copper wire was used to create this whimsical figure. Twisted copper-wire hair complements the brightly painted body.

Shirley Kinney

Shirley Kinney had been making and selling dolls, with heads made of modeling clay, for ten years before she discovered gourds. Then, when she was taken to a gourd farm and saw all the various shapes and sizes, she says, "I felt all the immense possibility inside that golden shape. At home I added clay faces, arms, and legs, and turned those wonderful gourds into faeries, gnomes, and aliens."

Shirley explains that she has started growing her own gourds and now has racks and racks of them. Most dolls are made with a wire armature, using the gourd as the body; the head, hands, and feet are made from clay. The gourd body defines the character of the doll. To her surprise, the doll doesn't always end up the way she wants it to, but the way the gourd seems to choose to fashion itself.

And the Beet Goes On, *Shirley Kinney*

Mahé, *David Roseberry*

Spirit Doll with Crystals, *Heather Hogan*

Pjs, *Dawn Schiller*

ADDING ARMS & LEGS 51

Pansy, *Linda Noblitt*

Joy, *Kristi Dial*

Beth McClure

Beth McClure has been an artist since she received her first box of crayons. Since that early beginning, she has been primarily a watercolorist, later delving into mixed media. She encountered gourds as a possibility for fresh ideas while exploring other dimensions for her art. When she began working with gourds, she was amazed to find they gave her so much direction. "The particular piece I get involved with," she says, "literally guides me to each and every embellishment, from the smallest to the largest, which takes me on a journey I sometimes can't even articulate."

Keeper of the Keys, *Beth McClure. Photo by the artist.*

Madonna 1, *Beth McClure. Photo by the artist.*

ADDING ARMS & LEGS   53

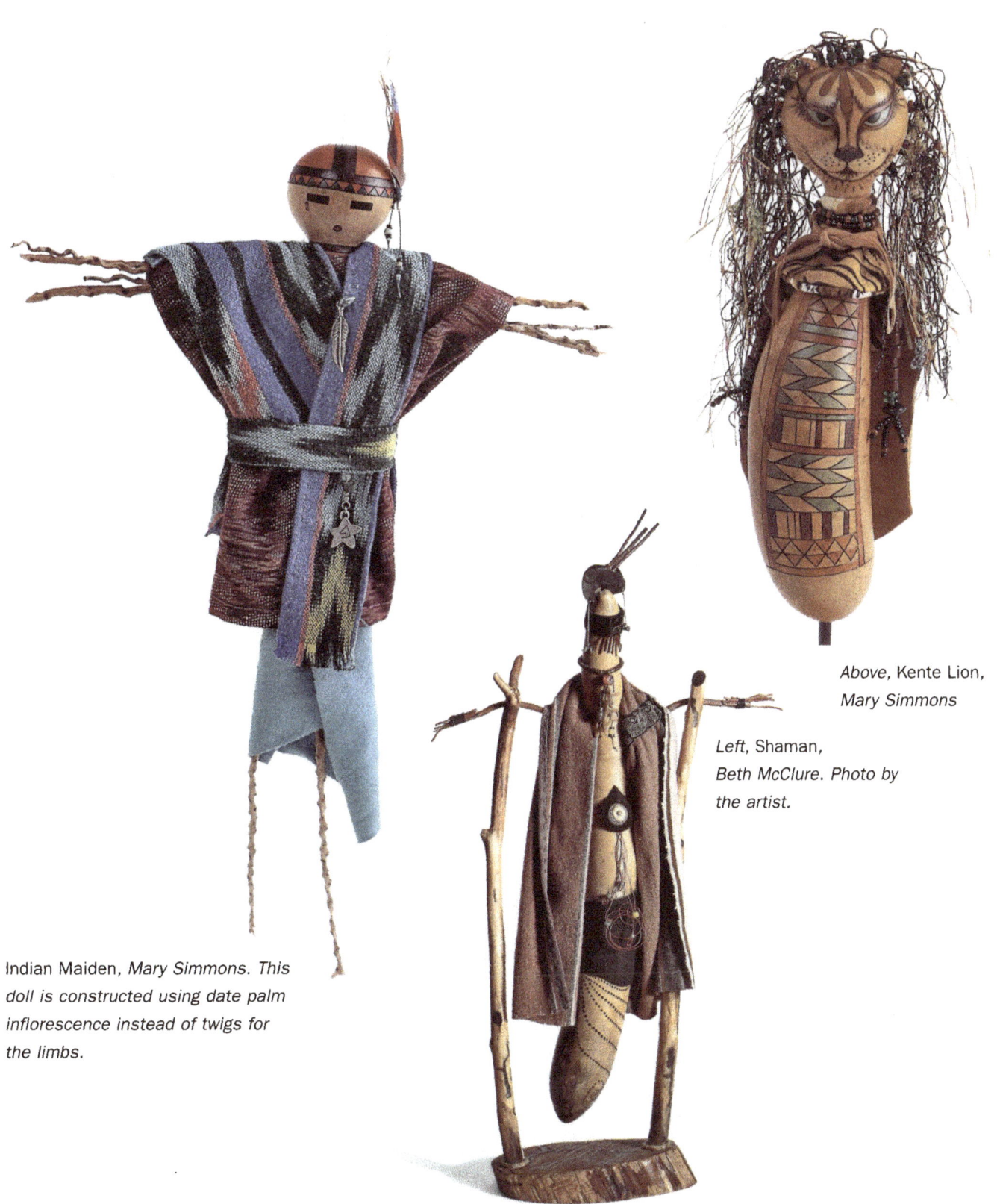

Above, Kente Lion, *Mary Simmons*

Left, Shaman, *Beth McClure. Photo by the artist.*

Indian Maiden, *Mary Simmons.* This doll is constructed using date palm inflorescence instead of twigs for the limbs.

Melissa Erhart

Melissa Erhart first encountered gourds at an apple farm, where she saw a finished gourd. When she got home, she investigated gourd crafting on the Internet, and, she says, "I was off to a brand-new playground for my heart and soul."

"With gourds," explains Melissa, "You could say we converse. I know this may sound silly, but I allow the gourd to lead me in the right direction." Although the gourd may first suggest one idea for a project, frequently it changes midcourse, and she is forced to go along another path altogether.

"Gourd shopping is more fun than any other shopping," she says. "I get quite excited when I come across a gourd that has its own character, so it seems to jump out at me. I do feel a special bond with gourds. I do feel their connection with the earth, with God, and with the human race."

Talking with God, *Melissa Erhart*

Suzanne Jordan

Suzanne Jordan, a mixed-media artist, used everything she could find when she was growing up "to make something." Now, gourds have brought together all the loose ends, and she is able to bring all her skills to her projects. Like nearly all gourd artists, she says that a project will sometimes take on its own voice as it flows from her heart to her hands. It is the voice of the doll that speaks to her and to which she responds. "Gourds have had their place in history and will continue long after I'm gone," she says. "We discover ourselves in our work, which often provides a deep connection with the projects we are working on." Suzanne gives all her spirit dolls a cleansing and a blessing after they are completed.

Tripod Spirit Doing a Rain Dance, *Suzanne Jordan*

Heather Hogan

Heather Hogan enjoys three-dimensional art. Working with gourds combines all the media she has worked with into one neat package. "I didn't have to throw a pot," she says. "Nature did it for me."

She feels that the gourd usually tells her what it wants to be. She looks for certain shapes, but then one particular gourd calls out to be a doll of a different kind. It seems that even when an image is in her mind, what the gourd wants to be still wins out in the end.

"I am lucky to live near a gourd farm," she says. "I always pick out my own gourds. It's like I have an invisible divining rod that waves over a pile of gourds and lights on the perfect ones. I like making dolls for friends that speak to their own personalities. When I make them for sale, it is interesting to watch how the doll and the new owner make a connection as well."

Wyvern, *Heather Hogan*

PROJECT 3

Kitchen Witch

For this project, the selected gourd appeared to be leaning forward—perfect for riding on a wooden spoon. After wire limbs, the face, and clothing are added, the Kitchen Witch can sit comfortably on her perch high in the kitchen corner.

In most other examples, the materials used to create the limbs, such as wire and wood, are not altered. However, at times it is desirable to supplement these materials, such as by padding the wire limbs, as done here.

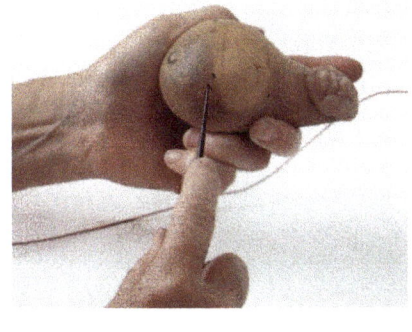

1. Choose a mini-gourd and fit with a clay face (see chapter 5). Make holes in the body of the gourd for the wire that will create the arms and legs.

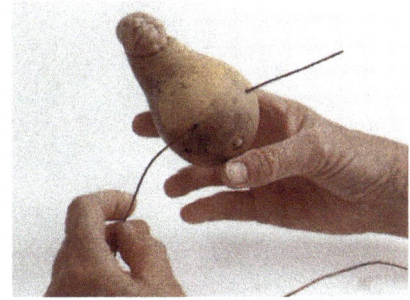

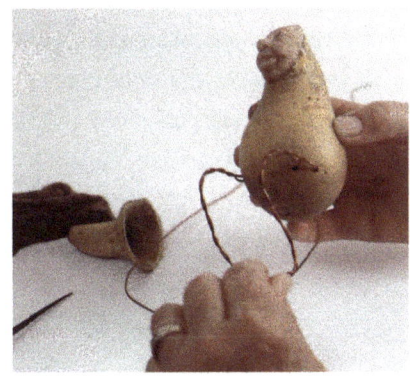

2 and **3.** Thread flexible copper wire through the body, and bend it back and twist it to create sturdy arms and legs.
Continued on page 58

58 ADDING LIMBS

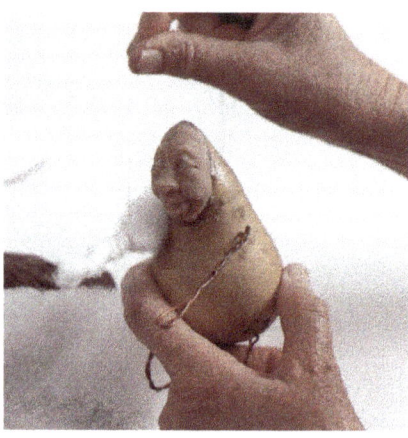

4. Wrap the wire with polyester batting.

7. Drill holes into the handle of a wooden kitchen spoon, for securing the witch by both hands and hips.

8. Dress the figure in a robe with the wire in place.

9. Drill holes into both ends of the spoon, and hang by fishing line. The Kitchen Witch is now ready to protect the household.

5. Wrap the polyester batting with strips of nylon stocking, to blend more with the color of the gourd and appropriate limbs.

6. Shape a hat from the top of a second mini-gourd.

Green Bug, *Mary Simmons*. *This figure uses a technique similar to that for constructing the* Kitchen Witch, *wrapping the wire limbs with fiber.*

Norwegian Kitchen Witch

While most people often associate witches with scary thoughts or evil intentions that usually haunt the imagination at Halloween, another image dates back to medieval Germany. This very benevolent spirit watches out for the welfare of the family, bringing good luck and warm feelings to the household. In popular folklore today, the Kitchen Witch is associated with the Norwegian culture, where she is the traditional symbol of good fortune in the home. According to legend, if the Kitchen Witch is near, cakes and breads will be perfect, milk won't sour, and pots won't boil over. Harmony will prevail throughout the house as long as she is there to keep the evil spirits at bay.

DOLLS WITH ARTICULATED JOINTS

While the figures just presented have arms and legs, they are largely intended to be secure and not moved, even when they are made of bendable wire. These figures are usually mounted on bases, and the limbs are posed in a way that complements their expression.

A very different dimension is added when the limbs are specifically designed to be moved. Suddenly the figure is not just something to be looked at, but rather to be held and manipulated, creating a bond between the object and the owner.

Dolls with movable parts date back to ancient times. The oldest examples were found in Greece in temples dedicated to Demeter and Persephone. Some have also been found in Egyptian tombs. We can only guess as to the purpose of these figures, but they are so distinct from other examples of statuettes or rigid figures that it is tempting to assume a special human connection was involved.

Different techniques can be used to attach limbs so that they can be moved. Each limb can be pegged, or attached to the body independently, or two opposing limbs can be connected with a wire or cord that extends through the body. Both of these techniques can be used when making gourd dolls.

PROJECT 4

Doll with Articulated Joints

This small doll can be built from a small bottle gourd and sections of a dipper-gourd handle. Because the shell of some handles is quite thin or brittle, the joints are reinforced with wooden beads.

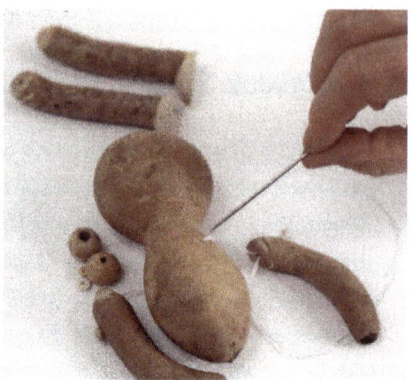

1. Select small ends of dipper gourds to complement the body of a mini–bottle gourd. The cut ends are reinforced by gluing beads of the correct diameter for both shoulders and hips. The beads are then sanded so that they fit the gourd body.

Linda Eichwald's jointed doll dressed in clothing and scarf. This is a variation on the doll shown in the steps on (these) pages 60–61. She used leather strips to connect and secure the limbs to the body.

2. Poke holes with a leather awl for the arms and legs. Secure a small bead at the end of heavy dental floss or waxed linen, and thread the needle through one arm, the body, and the second arm. Add a second bead, bring the needle back through the arm, and tie securely to the thread at the shoulder joint. (This hides the cut ends of the floss within the shoulder joint.)

DOLLS WITH ARTICULATED JOINTS 61

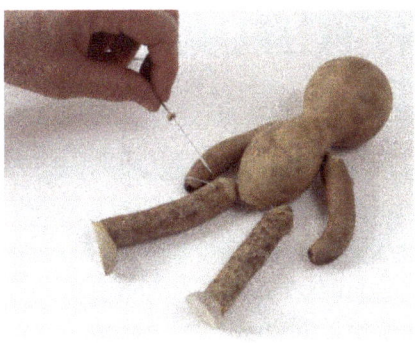

3. Repeat this process to attach the legs. Feet of half-round "wood robin eggs" (obtained at craft stores) are glued into place.

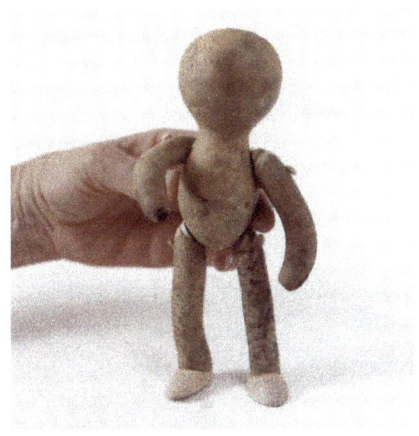

4. Here's the final assembled doll.

Mary Wojeck

Mary Woject first saw gourds as dippers at a springhouse. Since then, she has gone on to create hundreds of objects from gourds, including masks, animals, bowls, and lamps. She makes dolls out of specially selected mini–bottle gourds. The movable limbs are cut from the handles of dipper gourds and attached with bamboo skewers. She prefers to use natural materials whenever possible. For example, she often creates hair out of shredded bark.

Gourd doll, with gourd arms and legs,
Mary Wojeck

DOLLS WITH ARTICULATED COMPLEX JOINTS

In response to the challenge of making a much more movable doll, several artists have looked for ways to create figures with elbows and knees. This involves a quest to find perfectly matching stems of dipper gourds for arms and legs, as well as a solution to joining these pieces together in such a way that the soft gourd shell will not shatter.

Jigger Dolls

This form of doll is usually associated with eastern North America, ranging from Canada to Appalachia, although it probably originated in Germany in the seventeenth century. These peg dolls (the joints were constructed with pegs) were traditionally made of pine or linden wood. They were often carried by Dutch traders, gaining the name "Dutch dolls."

Closely related to the marionette, the jigger doll is a loosely jointed doll that combines the function of a musical instrument with a figure. The operator sits on a thin wooden board that extends in front of him or her. By means of a stick attached to a hole in the back, the doll is suspended so that the feet just touch the end of the board. Tapping on the board causes the feet of the doll to bounce and the arms to swing in rhythm to the music being played or sung. This toy, also called "Limber Jack" or "Dancing Dan," was very popular at the time of traveling minstrel shows in the nineteenth century, and the lively tapping and swinging of the doll's body was often imitated by performers and dancers at gatherings in mountain communities.

Limber Jill, *Jill Walker.* By combining pieces of dowel with the stem end of a bottle gourd, Jill Walker created this imaginative dancing partner. A wood dowel was put through the body of the gourd at chest level to mount the screws for the arms, and a carved block of wood was glued into the base to attach the legs. The handle that is attached permanently to the back of the gourd is also mounted into the dowel that connects the arms. In this way, all the joints are reinforced, enabling Limber Jill *to dance quite a jig!*

PROJECT 5

Dancing Dan

Dancing Dan can be constructed from parts of many gourds, starting with a small bottle gourd for the body. Although limbs can be fastened to the gourd body in many ways, a single cord connects the arm and leg on each side of the body here. This seems to hold the leg in a relatively snug position against the gourd body.

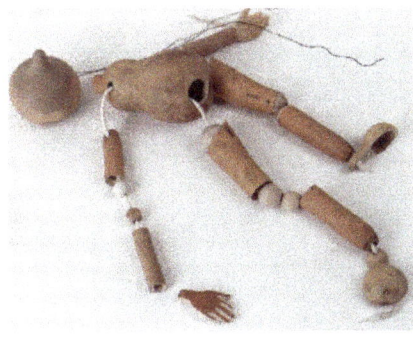

1. Find suitable gourds to create the body, head, arms, and legs. Carve the hands out of thick gourd scraps and sand them so that the wrists fit snugly into the arms. Cut a very small gourd in half to create feet. Glue a small round of a dipper gourd to the top of the body to create a neck; a wire connects the head, through the body, to the crotch between the legs. (Although a bit awkward, this arrangement allows for the head to turn and move.)

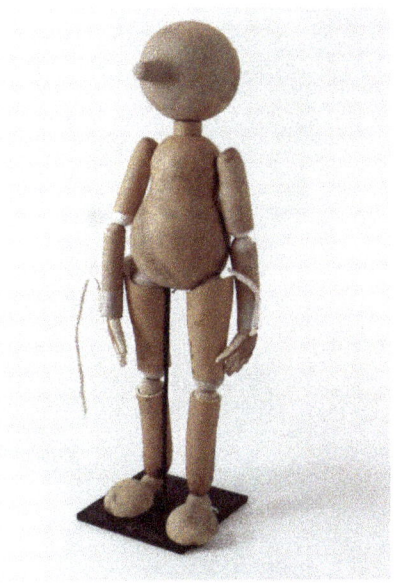

2. Thread a nylon cord from the wrist, through the arm, down the body, and through the leg, ending with a knot hidden in the shoe. Drilled wooden beads fitted at each end of the sections of the arms and legs provide very flexible joints.

3. To bring this puppet to life, secure a dowel into a hole in the middle of the back of the body. Hold the puppet so that the feet are lightly touching a length of flexible wood. While sitting at the other end of the wood piece, tap the wood to cause the puppet to dance.

MARIONETTES

By removing the rod from the back and attaching strings to the top of the head, wrists, and knees, Dancing Dan can easily be turned into a marionette. Additional controls can be added at different points on the body and limbs, but it is best to start with fewer movements before adding more.

Marionette with movable joints, Betty Finch

Double marionette, one side, Jan Seeger

Marionette created with multicolored gourd "balls," Sue Westhues

CHAPTER FOUR
Dolls with Gourd Heads

WIRE-ARMATURE DOLLS

While some artists use the gourd as the body or foundation of the doll and add a head made of another material, others use the gourd as the head and then create a separate body using wire, cord, or something else. The resulting figure has very flexible limbs and can be embellished to portray any type of image.

According to gourd artist Kris Mangliers, in some places in Africa women would make these dolls from scraps of material and hide messages of protection within their wrapped bodies. They would then give these dolls to their children to protect them while the mothers were working in the fields.

Gourdy Andy, *Linda Noblitt*

WIRE-ARMATURE DOLLS **67**

Simple wire armature, Cathy Burton. This basic framework illustrates how to create a structure for both the shoulder and hip areas that provides a bit of stability for the extended limbs.

African wire doll, Kris Mangliers

PROJECT 6

Jesters

This project provides one way to take advantage of the extremely flexible, pose-able limbs of this style of doll. The head can be left plain, or it can be painted or embellished with clay to create features.

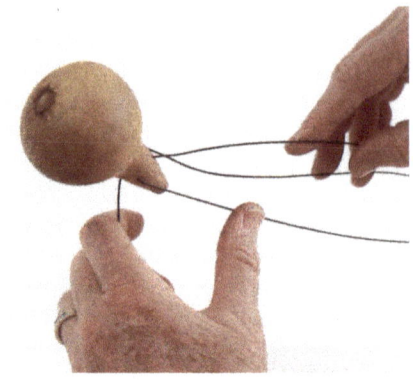

1. Make four holes in the neck of the gourd. Cut two lengths of flexible craft wire, one for the arms and the other for the body and legs. The wire for the arms should be approximately five times the length of the arm, and the wire for the body should be approximately five times the length from the neck to the toe. Thread the wires through the holes, and then wrap around the base of the gourd once to make sure the head will be stable. Bend the wires for the arms so that there is a loop for hands, and then bring the ends back to the center portion of the body. (Some artists prefer to add molded-clay hands or beads for hands. These elements should be added at this time.) Twist the arm wires slightly to provide strength for the arms.

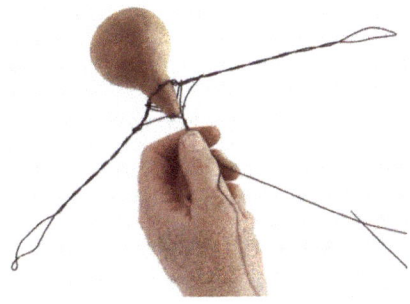

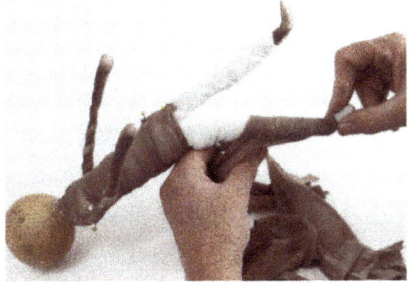

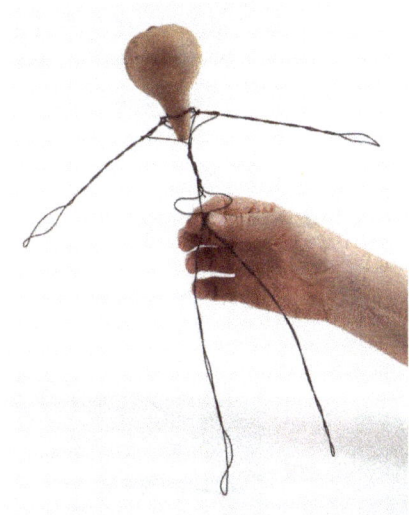

4. Wrap the wire limbs with cotton batting, and hold in place with string or thread. Cover the batting with strips of nylon stocking, and secure in place. Add more batting or wrap the entire figure with strips of yarn or cloth until you get the shape you want.

5. Dress the doll as desired. In this case, the faces of the jesters were created with additional clay and then painted, hair of uncombed fleece was glued in place, and the figures were dressed. One jester is carrying a rod embellished with a laughing clay face.

2 and 3. Twist the other wire slightly, and bring around the arms, to create a shoulder girdle. Then continue twisting the wires to create a body and hip area. Make a loop for the feet, and bring the ends back, twisting to form the legs.

DOLLS WITH CLOTH BODIES

Throughout the world, dolls have been created using cloth bodies, topped by heads made of wood, ivory, ceramic, porcelain, and more recently, plastic. Carved wooden heads are the most prevalent, and they may have been used often to replace other heads that broke. The advantage of this type of doll is that the body could be used many times with different heads to create various figures. Likewise, new bodies could be made to give new life to worn-out ones. Dolls with simple carved heads were very popular among early American settlers, most likely as a substitute for the more expensive china dolls. Figures with gourd heads attached to cloth bodies have been used in Africa since very early times.

The body can be as simple as a pillow or made more complex with articulated limbs. Many cloth-doll bodies are available readymade at craft stores.

Options to consider are whether to add gourd pieces for the arms and legs, and how to connect the gourd to the body.

Betsy (Crown of Thorns), *Pat Duncan*

Gourd-head doll, *Lelia Thomas*

Gourd doll from Mali. Dick and Beany Wezelman collection.

DOLLS WITH CLOTH BODIES

Appalachian gourd dolls. Ginger Summit collection.

Ardith Willner

Ardith Willner, a floral designer, selects her own gourds at gourd farms. She is an accomplished seamstress, so combining gourd with cloth body came naturally. She looks for just the right gourds for what she calls her "squash blossoms" and affixes them to the main gourd piece. The velvet outfit and jewelry suggest traditional Native American dress.

Running Deer, *Ardith Willner*

72 DOLLS WITH GOURD HEADS

African soft doll, Jill Walker

Hope, *Mimi Kirchner*

Mimi Kirchner

Mimi Kirchner works in all kinds of media and specializes in dollmaking. When she first saw gourds, they looked like perfect doll heads to her. She tries to paint a face that matches the gourd and then creates dresses to complete the personality. When creating one of her dolls, she carefully turns the gourd around to discover the character it already expresses.

Saide, *Mimi Kirchner. Photo by the artist.*

Jane, *Mimi Kirchner. Photo by the artist.*

Celeste, *Mimi Kirchner*

74 DOLLS WITH GOURD HEADS

Out of My Gourd, *Linda Noblitt*

Gourdy Mollie, *Linda Noblitt*

Gourdy Guys, *Linda Noblitt*

CHAPTER FIVE
Addition of Clay Parts

Often artists find gourds that have the perfect shape for the body of the figure, but in order to create the character and expression of the spirit hidden within, they add features of clay.

L'oeuf, *Dawn Schiller*

USING CLAY IN MOLDS

For crafters who are not comfortable with sculpting a face, there are many molds and clays on the market today that can easily be adapted for this task. The molds come in a variety of sizes and shapes, with many different facial expressions. You'll find everything from a smiling child to a somber old crone. Simply push air-drying clay into these molds to create an assortment of faces for future projects.

Feather Princess, *with clay face, Deborah Moskowitz. This face was attached to the gourd with wireings.*

Using Molds to Make Faces and Hands and Feet

1. First lightly dust the mold with cornstarch for easy release.

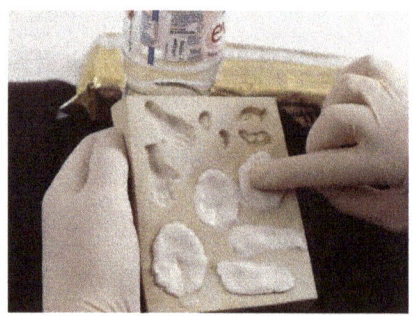

2. Push the modeling clay into the mold. If necessary, add a little water to the clay to make sure it is pliable enough to get into all the impressions in the mold. Then, with your finger and a little more moisture, rub the clay into the mold.

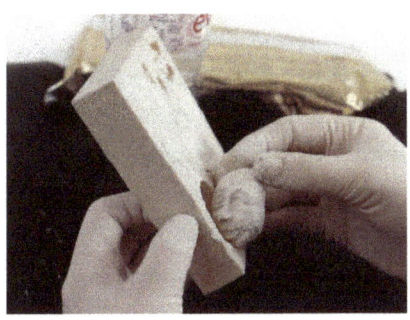 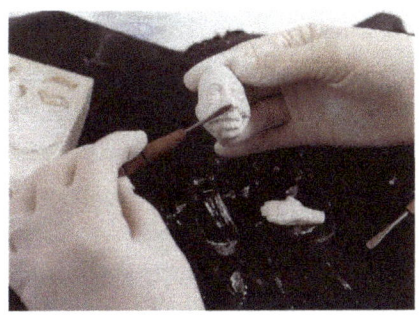 

3. When the clay has partially dried, carefully remove it from the mold by pushing out from the back of the mold.

4. While the clay is still pliable, you can easily resculpt the features to add wrinkles, a smile, or any other desired expression. Often these molds include hands and feet in a variety of sizes. These additions can enhance the doll.

5. After you remove the hands and feet from the mold, you can reshape them before they dry. If you wish, the hands can be shaped to grasp an object and the feet made/modified to fit a mounting base.

Attaching the Face

After making several faces of clay, find a gourd that matches the size, shape, and mood of the features of one of the faces. The clay can be sanded to fit the curvature of the gourd, or the gourd can be cut out so that the face can be inset.

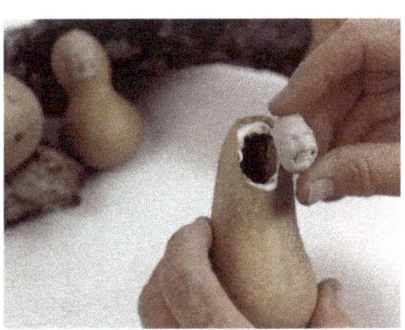 

1. After the face is dry, trace around the shape. Cut the hole in the gourd slightly smaller than the clay face. Make a bevel on the edge that's slighter wider on the outer edge of the cut so that you'll have more surface for gluing the clay. That will prevent the clay from being pushed accidentally into the gourd.

2. When the glue is dry, fill in the edge around the face with a small roll of clay or add embellishments to hide the seam.

Betsy Roberts

Betsy Roberts says she loves "to tinker, try out new things, and play with gourds...they have touched my soul." "I start my dolls at the body. I next find the perfect face (at least I think so at that moment). I then start the feathering process, one feather at a time. I work with them while their bodies are alone, standing up on a holder. As the face develops, I let my imagination go to other embellishments I have, to tie the head to the body and make them one. My dolls have to direct me every step of the way."

Bird-Watcher, *Betsy Roberts*

Blue Goddess, *Betsy Roberts*

USING CLAY IN MOLDS **79**

Red Spirits, *Betsy Roberts*

Sleeping Princess, *Betsy Roberts*

Leopard Man, *Betsy Roberts*

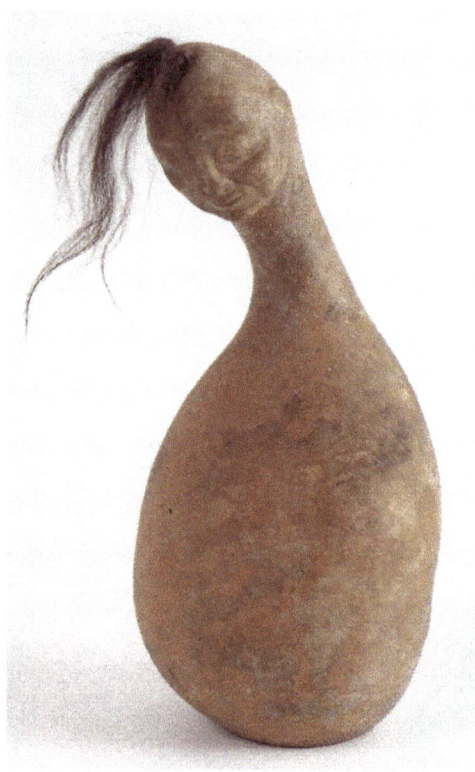

Above, gourd figure with sculpted clay face, Betty Finch

SCULPTING CLAY FACES

Because the molds come in a limited range of sizes, artists often just sculpt the clay directly on the gourd shell. Any air-drying clay is suitable for this. Lightly roughen the surface of the gourd first, to ensure that the clay will adhere to the gourd (see the "Stacked Dolls: Mother & Children" project in chapter 6).

Colleen Huff

Colleen Huff's gourd dolls "often take on the many faces from my travels," she says. "In creating a doll, a slight turn in the angle of the head will jolt a visual memory, and from that moment the figure just tells me what it needs. The final stage of each piece is never the same—the dolls are like portraits of individuals. With gourds, I feel the oneness of humanity. I love working on a canvas that has been used throughout so many different cultures."

Right, Asian Grace Series, Colleen Huff. Photo by the artist.

Kris Mangliers

Artist Kris Mangliers was asked to participate in an open studio with a potter and a basket weaver. They wanted a project that would integrate all three earth elements, so she chose the *Maiden with Burden Basket* piece. The maiden's body is part of a snake gourd, her face is clay, the hair is horsetail, and the base she stands on is made from hand-built stoneware. The burden basket is woven with wild iris and seaweed.

Kris integrates her basketry techniques into her gourd projects. She tries to select gourds with unusual shapes and markings, even cracks, because they offer more of a challenge. She first made wire dolls as a project at a conference, and since then has found working with wire to be an extremely flexible and favorable technique for doll construction. "I love the whimsical motion, their sacred legend, and the fact that I can use up scraps of material and yarn," she says.

Gift Snatcher, *Sherry Goshen. This figure is made from several gourds, with a clay head, cloth hands, and cloth and leather feet. The upper legs are gourds. "The Gift Snatcher is the one who steals presents—you know, you buy gifts and when you go to wrap them, they can't be found. You didn't misplace them; this little guy has taken them."*

Maiden with Burden Basket, *Kris Mangliers*

82 ADDITION OF CLAY PARTS

Gwenivere, *Carolyn Potter. Photo by Cori.*

Kristi Dial

Although she studied art in college, Kristi Dial didn't start doing her own artwork until 1995, when she took a class in basketry and gourd crafting. "My spirit seems to become so centered and at peace when I hold a gourd. The gourd and I talk to each other. Sometimes the gourd speaks first, and other times I do the talking. Very rarely do we disagree.

"I have a spiritual connection with Native Americans, and I strive to honor their culture and history. I want people to look at my shamans and sense the strength and wisdom of the elder. For me, gourds are nature's canvas, and I want to honor the gourd. I want the viewer to see that it is a gourd as well. I believe the gourd needs to be honored with simplicity."

The Elder, *Kristi Dial*

Lynne Bunt

Lynne Bunt discovered gourds after leaving the corporate world. She feels that in the artistic process, she and the gourd collaborate with each other. When making her dolls, Lynn always uses the gourd as the body, adding the face, which she shapes from clay, and dressing it in natural materials. For her, working with a canvas that is part of the earth is sacred.

Left, Crone, *Lynne Bunt. Photo by George Post.*
Right, Grandmother, *Lynne Bunt*

Gourd Shaman, *Lynne Bunt. Photo by George Post.*

Julie Lovejoy

Artist Julie Lovejoy explains how she selects gourds: "First, as I paw through bins of dried gourds, I wait for some to pop out and say, 'Me! You can't leave without me!' Those gourds automatically go into the 'take' pile. I also have ideas percolating in the back of my mind about my next piece, so I look for gourds that will make great body parts (heads, arms, etc.). My eye is attracted to gourds that are not perfect—scars add character to a piece." Julie is inspired by mystery and by the nature spirits in all their forms. Old faces hold a particular fascination for her, and she tries to create that sense of mystery in her work.

The Crone, *Julie Lovejoy*

Tituba's Song, *Julie Lovejoy*

Dances with Gourds, *Julie Lovejoy*

USING CLAY FOR LIMBS & OTHER SHAPES

Pieces of clay can be added to the gourd body to create limbs as well as just the face. For example, with the *Beggar God* figure, a roll of clay depicts the arms and the withered leg. Clay hands and feet made from molds were also added.

Legend of Li-T'ieh-Kuai, the Beggar God

In China today, the bottle gourd is recognized as a symbol of herbal medicine and healing. The origin of this symbol can be traced to an ancient legend about Li-T'ieh-Kuai, the oldest of the eight immortal gods and the patron deity of medicine. He is frequently depicted as a crippled beggar with a crutch in his hand and a bottle gourd tied to his sash.

According to legend, however, he began as a handsome young noble who studied philosophy and strived for immortality. One day he instructed a young disciple to watch over his body as his spirit went to visit Lao-tzu at the Sacred Mountain. When his spirit returned to his body many days later, he found that it had been burned to ashes. Anxious to find another physical form, Li's spirit entered the body of a beggar who had recently died. When he realized his new misshapen form, he pleaded with the gods for help.

Lao-tzu responded by giving him a crutch and a bottle gourd of magic herbs to cure mortals. So by day he wandered the streets as a healing mendicant, and at night his spirit entered the bottle gourd, which contained a magical world of comfort and peace. He is readily recognizable as a lame unkempt figure, with a black face, untamed hair, and a wild beard, carrying an iron crutch and a gourd.

Beggar God, *Ginger Summit*. The arms, withered leg, hands, and feet are made of clay. The face was wood-burned. She used decoupaged fabric for the robe and glued disheveled hair (donated by Ginger's dog) into place.

Mary Driussi-Yaber

While researching symbols in Mexican basketry, Mary Driussi-Yaber discovered gourds. She visits gourd farms and spends a long time choosing the right gourds for her pieces. Mary sometimes discovers a gourd that calls to her, although the finished piece may not turn out at all like the original idea.

Mexican Musician, *Mary Driussi-Yaber*

Native American spirit doll,
Mary Driussi-Yaber

88 ADDITION OF CLAY PARTS

Dancing Native American figure in traditional attire, Mary Driussi-Yaber

Inuit, *Dawn Schiller*

USING CLAY FOR LIMBS & OTHER SHAPES   **89**

Prayer Hands, *Beverly Shamana.*
Photo by George Post.

The Golfer, *Pat Duncan*

Figure with clay parts, *Lavonne Hall*

CHAPTER SIX
Stacked Dolls

COMBINING GOURDS

Most gourds presented in earlier chapters consist of single gourds embellished with decorative clothing or supplemented with other materials for limbs and sometimes the entire body. The next step involves combining gourds or pieces of gourds (stacking gourds) to create more elaborate figures. Not only does this expand the shape and dimension of a single gourd, but the resulting figure becomes quite sculptural, taking advantage of the grace of a single gourd plus the myriad curvatures and textures that exist on other shells as well.

The kokeshi doll of Japan provides a good introduction to the possibilities of combining parts of gourds to create a figure.

Fu Hi, *Jo Cooley*

KOKESHI DOLLS, KACHINAS & OTHER DOLLS

Kokeshi Dolls

Dolls are important in a number of traditions in Japanese society. One popular style of doll is the kokeshi doll, which dates back at least 300 years. Some of the dolls are playthings, but usually they are used in festivals and shrines, and may have had religious significance at one time. Historically, mothers cared for the doll to bring protection to their children. Beginning in the eighteenth century, kokeshi dolls were placed by the head of a newborn baby, both to confuse any evil spirits and to protect the child and bring good health. The true kokeshi is made of turned wood, ranging from 2 inches to 2 feet (5 cm to 60 cm) high. The body is stylized as a cylinder, topped by a round head, which often can be turned. Some dolls are draped with cloth or paper in the style of the kimono worn in the local culture or period. Most, however, are painted, and specific motifs vary by region.

Two special holidays are celebrated in Japan when kokeshi dolls assume great importance. The most significant is Hina Matsuri, on the third day of the third month (March 3), which is the Girls' Festival or Honorable Small Doll Festival. Each house displays a collection of fifteen dolls in ancient costumes on a special set of shelves. The dolls represent the old royal court with emperor and empress as well as newer members of the court. The display shows the importance of marriage and family life, reverence for the ruling house, and the value of maintaining social order. These dolls are displayed only at this particular festival, and families take special pride in the quality of the dolls and the completeness of the display.

The other holiday, on the fifth day of the fifth month (May 5), is the Boys' Festival. A set of warrior dolls may be displayed on this occasion. These dolls represent strength, bravery, and patriotism.

PROJECT 7

Kokeshi Doll

Although kokeshi dolls are traditionally made of carved wood, gourds can be used with equal success. Kokeshi figures can be plain or extremely fancy, but it's best to start with two main components: a body and a head.

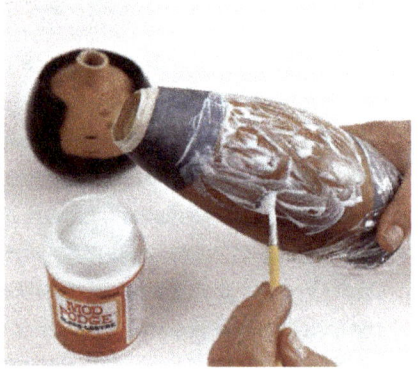

1. Select two gourd pieces, one for the body and a smaller round piece for the head. Drill a hole in the top of the gourd body, and shape it to fit the neck of the head securely.

2. For this doll, the aim was to add a layer of hair by covering the head with another gourd. After cutting this gourd in the appropriate shape for hair (a sort of wig or hairpiece), the opening in the hairpiece was not large enough to accommodate the head. To help make it fit, a section was then removed from the hairpiece and it was fitted around the head. Then the outer gourd (hairpiece) was glued back together. The seam was covered with clay to make sure it appeared smooth.

3. The robe, made of rice paper from Japan, bears a lovely gourd design. Because traditional Japanese costumes consist of many layers, another paper forms the collar and undergarment. Now paint a thick layer of white glue on the gourd body.

KOKESHI DOLLS, KACHINAS & OTHER DOLLS

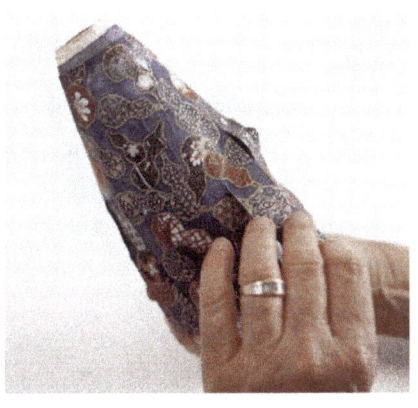

4. Cut the paper for the outer garment carefully, including slits where the paper will overlap to conform to the shape of the gourd. Carefully put the cut paper in place.

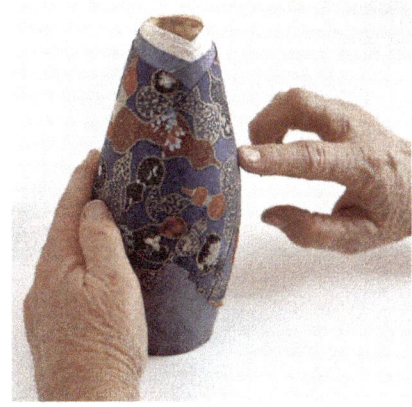

5. Rub the paper to remove any air bubbles and to smooth out the surface.

7. A thin gold ribbon is added as accent along the edges of the outer garment. When the glue is completely dry, protect the body of the gourd with a lacquer or polyurethane.

6. The traditional kokeshi doll has a head that can be turned. If the neck of the gourd head is not long enough to extend into the body, carve a cork to fit snugly into the neck of the bottle gourd and glue it in place. Then cut the hole in the gourd body to fit securely around the cork.

Jo Cooley

Jo Cooley, a former ceramics artist, prefers the medium of gourds. "My favorite part of creating my gourd dolls is finding pieces and putting them together," she says. "My gourds can have up to five pieces on them. Sometimes they stay in that state for quite a while before I add color and other embellishments."

Shin Mu, *Jo Cooley*

Melody, *Jo Cooley*

KOKESHI DOLLS, KACHINAS & OTHER DOLLS 95

Japanese stacked dolls, Lynette Dawson

Maia, Jo Cooley

Stacked-gourd figure, Lynette Dawson

Thena Trygstad

Thena Trygstad focuses on constructing objects from gourds. Her interest in gourds began when a friend gave her a gourd plant, which then grew thirty huge gourds. Not knowing what to do with them, she attended a gourd show, and, as she says, "the rest is history." Gourds definitely speak to her, in her garden and on her worktable. "Not every project I conceptualize comes together as I originally envision," Thena says. "A partially constructed project can sit on my table for months because it doesn't like how it was started. Then it will speak to me and often ends up as an entirely different character."

Tomte, *Thena Trygstad*

Wizard Wartsanall, *Thena Trygstad*

PROJECT 8

Stacked Dolls: Mother & Children

This project developed from a simple challenge of making a figure with a gourd body and attached arms and legs. But the gourd demanded a gourd dress rather than one made of fabric, and the curves in the arms asked to be holding something precious. The result is this stacked-doll project in which a mother is united with her children.

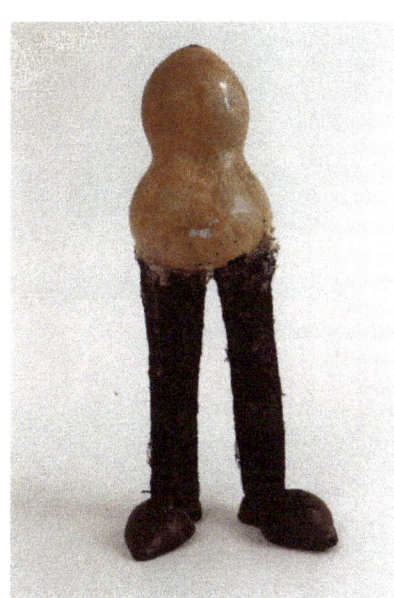

1. A small bottle gourd makes the torso of this composite stacked doll. Legs of dipper gourds are attached to feet cut from a mini-gourd. The legs are covered with cheesecloth and painted black.

2. Fit undergarments made of cotton to the body.

3. Cut a large bottle gourd to form the dress over the body.

4. To add more height, position a second gourd over the body to become the bodice of the clothing.

5. Additional gourds become the head and arms.

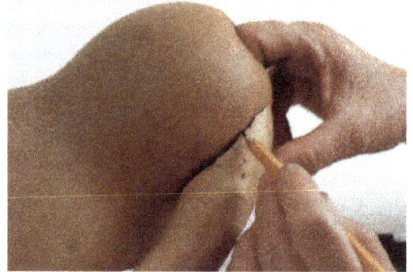

6. Cut and shape the arms to conform to the curvature of the bodice, and trace the seam onto the gourd.

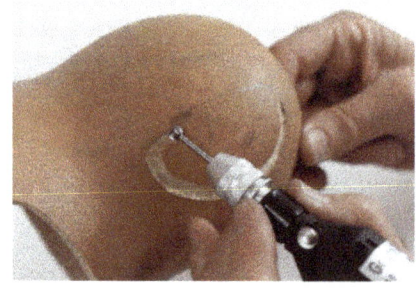

7. With a hobby drill, groove a channel into the bodice.

KOKESHI DOLLS, KACHINAS & OTHER DOLLS   99

8. Glue the arm in place.

9. Secure with tape until dry. The hands are carved out of mini-gourds and fit into the ends of the arms. (See the "Spirit of Summer" project in chapter 8.)

10. To create a face on the gourd head, first roughen the area where the facial features will be with sandpaper or a sanding disc on a hobby drill.

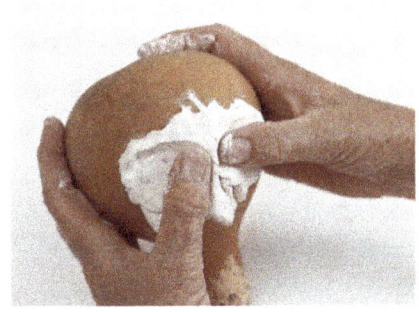

11. Mold air-drying clay onto the gourd, carefully shaping the eyebrows, cheeks, nose, and chin.

12. Add lips with two small rolls of clay.

13. Use clay tools to finely sculpt facial details.

14. Smooth the entire face before the clay is completely dry.

15. When dry, decoupage a paper dress. The paper used here resembles a vintage cotton print. The apron was painted, and a collar was fashioned of lace. Glue in place the hair of uncombed fleece, and paint the facial features with watercolors. This figure resembled a mother, so a baby was created out of a mini–bottle gourd, with the features molded out of clay. A daughter was created following the same steps as those for the mother.

See finished doll on page 97.

Crow Mother, *Bonnie Gibson*.
Collection of Sher Elliott-Widess.

Snake-Gourd Dolls

This popular style of gourd figure incorporates many elements described thus far, such as added pieces and clay faces. Frequently the body of the figure is a long slender form, cut from a snake gourd (dipper and banana gourds are also used). Snake-gourd dolls are often tipped in a position that requires that they be weighted and secured firmly to a base. Headdresses, clothing, and other decorative elements added to the body are usually representative of a particular culture and very traditional. Other accessories, such as pots and baskets, help to identify the festival or attribute being depicted.

Kachina Dolls

Kachina dolls, now more broadly associated with the Indians of the Southwest, are part of a rich tradition of the Hopi culture. Other Pueblo nations have adopted and incorporated them into their own belief systems and festivals. The word *kachina* refers to the supernatural beings in the Hopi worldview. Every aspect of the natural world is controlled by spirit beings, to which humans can appeal for health and survival. The kachinas represent the mediators or messengers by which humans communicate with the supernatural. The Hopi believe that in ancient times, the kachinas themselves took an active part in the festivals of the tribes. But gradually they withdrew and were represented by masked impersonators. When humans don the kachina masks and participate in sacred dances, however, it is felt that they actually do become part of the spirit world.

Only selected men are allowed to participate in these masked dances, and so in the kivas (ceremonial structures) they carve small figures to use in the religious instruction of the women and children. These carved figures, or kachina dolls, serve as symbols of beings in the sacred realm. Each is imbedded with specific patterns and designs to represent "real" kachinas. In addition to serving a religious function, these dolls help to pass on tribal memories in the form of storytelling. Thus, the dolls gradually acquired multiple meanings depending on the specific tribe of which they were a part. Even though the specific meaning of the individual kachina may vary, it remains a religious icon and is not a toy or plaything.

Bonnie Gibson

Artist Bonnie Gibson has received a great deal of satisfaction from creating things, using tools, and working with her hands. Although she had experimented with many different kinds of media, she immediately recognized that gourds have great potential and would allow her to integrate all the skills and tools she had used.

Having lived in the Southwest for thirty years, Bonnie has great respect for the Native American traditions and cultures, and often finds inspiration from them for her own work. "Working with Native or other cultural themes presents some ethical challenges," she says. "It is sometimes difficult to know where to draw the line between expressing an admiration for a culture and perhaps borrowing too heavily from it. My personal choice is to create items that are accurate in spirit but use nontraditional materials and presentations."

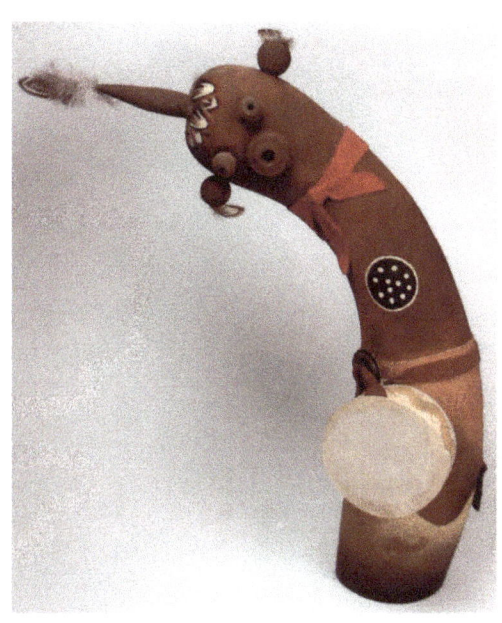

Mud Man, *Bonnie Gibson*

Counting Coup, *Bonnie Gibson. This piece is made from a snake gourd, an egg gourd, and added gourd items for the shield and headdress. Added embellishments include air-dried clay, fur, feathers, leather, wood, and bone beads.*

Marcia Sarianen

Marcia Sarianen, a self-taught artist, first encountered gourds at a festival near her home in southern California and later took a class. "The process of producing a doll allows for a wide range of creative possibilities," she says. "Working with gourds is an organic art. Gourds are nature's pottery. They are also a blank canvas with the potential for experimenting with a multitude of embellishment applications. Is anything out of bounds? For me, less is more."

Mary Simmons

Mary Simmons has worked with fiber and textile arts. Although she weaves and spins, she also enjoys basketry and quilting. Her grandfather grew gourds in Santa Barbara, and she loved the different shapes and sizes. It wasn't until the 1980s, when Mary was experimenting with new basketry techniques, that she recognized other possibilities that gourds offered. When she first started working with them, she says, "It was love at first sight. I knew that I could combine all the things that I love into gourds—basketry, stitching, color, texture, and natural embellishments."

She tries to listen to each gourd. "The shape and the color of the gourd may push me in a direction. But more than that, each gourd does seem to have a spirit that knows what it wants to become. We have a dialogue.

"I have always loved folk-art dolls, and they tend to inspire the birth of my own dolls. When working on a project, I start in one of two ways. I am challenged

Spirit Doll, *Marcia Sairanen*

Earth Momma, *Mary Simmons*

to use a textile, and try to create a doll that will be appropriate to that embellishment. Or I first design a face and body, and then search for the special items that will complete the doll. I have large collections of shells, moss, pods, twigs, and fabrics and trims from secondhand stores.

"The sacredness in gourds comes from two sources. One is the connection with nature. There is a feeling of belonging to the earth and a true connection with all living things. The second is the connection to people of other cultures all over the world. I feel a strong connection to people, past and present, from cultures different from my own when I'm working on a gourd. There is a sacred feeling about being part of a global community."

Fan Dancer, *Mary Simmons*

Mermaid, *Mary Simmons*

Diana Tollenaar

Diana Tollenaar has always been involved with art, but after reading a gourd book, she changed from two-dimensional to three-dimensional projects. The gourd has offered endless possibilities in her new direction. She chooses gourds at local gourd farms and then searches for the right combinations to turn them into her "Spirit People." Each figure takes on an individual life, and she feels as if they are kindred spirits, which is why she calls them "Spirit People."

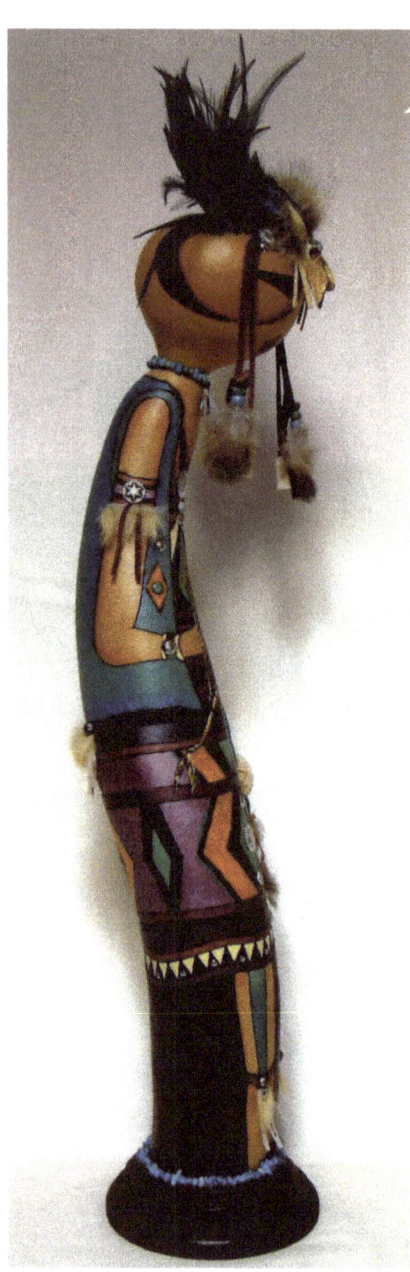

Snake-gourd spirit figure, Diana Tollenaar

Close-up view

KOKESHI DOLLS, KACHINAS & OTHER DOLLS 105

Kokopelli, *Judy Richie*. Photo by the artist.

Snake-gourd figure with headdress, Kathy Riker

Kouda, Keeper of the Gourds, *Gale Hurley. Photo by Raine Rodolph.*

She, *Gale Hurley. Photo by Raine Rodolph.*

Barbara Lewis

Artist Barbara Lewis works in a variety of media, but discovered in gourds a way to put all her studies in design and color to use. Since being introduced to gourds a few years ago, a whole new artistic world has opened up for her. "As I create each gourd figure," she says, "I feel like I'm creating a new person who is in some sense related to and a part of me. I feel that since a gourd is a natural design of nature, it is intrusive to force things into your work that do not enhance the natural feel of the gourd itself. Keeping gourds as natural as possible is a fitting way to say thank you for giving us this wonderful canvas."

Pot Woman, *Barbara Lewis. Photo by the artist.*

Plains Woman, *Barbara Lewis. Photo by the artist.*

CHAPTER SEVEN
Fiber Arts & Beading

WRAPPING, NETTING & WEAVING

Gourd scarecrow from Lombok, Indonesia. Knotless netting was worked around the body of the gourd. Collection of Ethnic Arts, Berkeley, California.

In places as far apart as Papua New Guinea and Africa, gourds have served as a foundation for coverings, such as wrapping, netting, and weaving, for hundreds of years. Each culture finds very different ways to combine its decorative techniques with gourds, and they have become central to rituals and ceremonies, as well as daily life.

Today, fiber artists carry on these traditions. Often the entire gourd is covered by netting, crochet, or weaving, but it is also possible to cover just portions of the gourd or to fill in openings.

After cutting and shaping the opening of the gourd, holes are drilled along the edges to attach the netting. Warp can also be strung across such an opening, which can then be filled with trapunto, or needle weaving.

WRAPPING NETTING & WEAVING 109

Navaho Weaver, *Fonda Haddad*. This dignified weaver and mother has black hair gathered at the back of her neck in a corded bun. Her garment is painted on, but her shawl, which attaches her baby to her back, was hand-loomed on a floor loom by Fonda (in another life, a weaver). The baby is secure and asleep in its own soft leather cradle. The loom is attached to the gourd with sticks and woven with waxed-linen warp and cotton threads.

Madonna Gourd Lady, *Fonda Haddad*. Here, the shape of the gourd lent itself to a Madonna. The simple lines were carved to create a feeling of reflection. It is stained with a dark-blue leather stain. A knotless netting in a soft drape of several combined yarns was used for the head and shoulder scarf. The couched basketry reeds are draped to emulate the layers of a flowing garment.

From Within, *Cookie Cala*

110 FIBER ARTS & BEADING

Three-Part Twining

In this sequence, gourd artist Cookie Cala explains how three weaving strands of different colors are twined to create a diagonal pattern along the body of the gourd. Twining is a form of weaving in which the weaver twists the strands around each other as they pass in front of two warp strands, or spokes, and behind one warp strand.

1. Weaving-strands A, B, and C are twined across the warp-strands (spokes) D, E, and F.

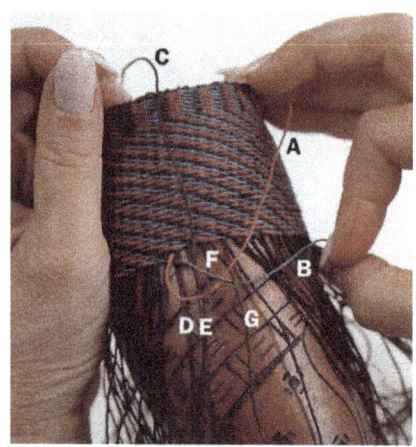

2. Weaving-strand A passes over warp-strands D and E and then under warp-strand F.

Weaving-strand B passes over warp-strands E and F and then under the adjacent strand G to the right of F.

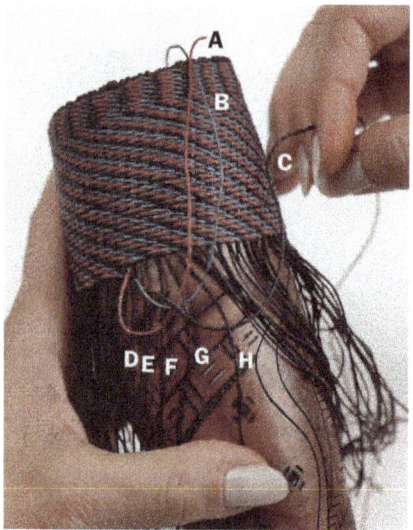

3. Weaving-strand C passes over warp-strands F and G and then under the adjacent strand H to the right of G.

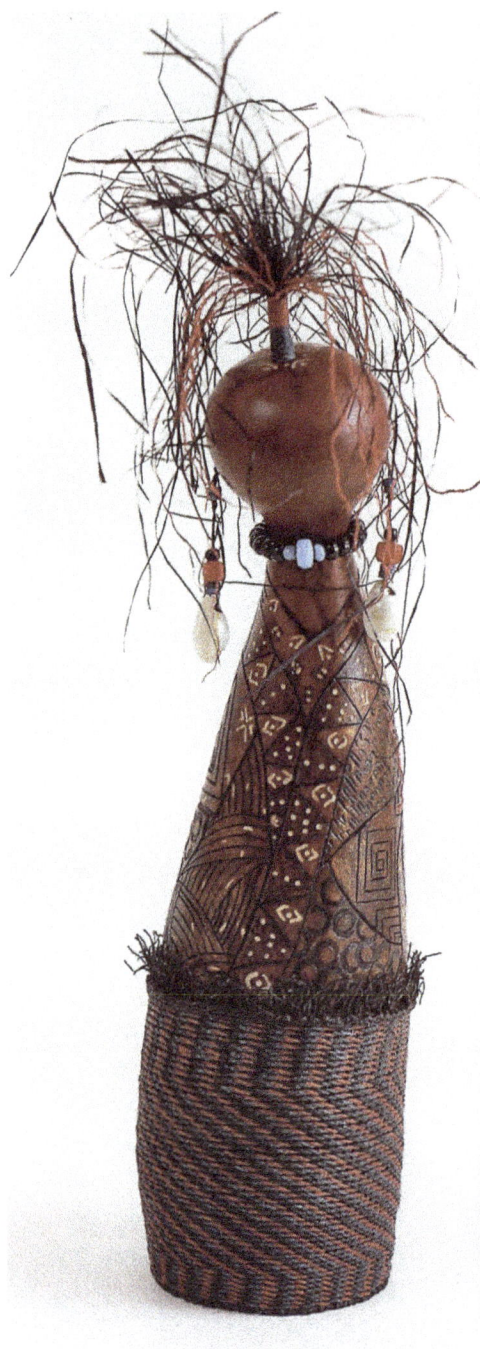

Night Out, *Cookie Cala. Three-part twining is woven around the gourd.*

Kathy Rousso

Kathy Rousso, a fiber artist who has lived in southeastern Alaska, learned to twist native materials into baskets and other pieces. Recently, she has been researching maguey-fiber textiles in Guatemala.

"I used netting techniques to embellish the dolls *Here* and *There*," she explains. "The doll *There* represents Guatemala, with looped maguey, while *Here* speaks to Alaska, with twined cedar. *Everywhere* is a mix of the two, including things from my bags of buttons and shells collected over the years."

Everywhere *(mix of Alaska and Guatemala)*, Kathy Rousso

Here *(Alaska)*, Kathy Rousso

There *(Guatemala)*, Kathy Rousso

Fiber Arts & Beading

Harry Hedgehog, *Lois Rainwater*

Lois Rainwater

Primarily a basket maker, Lois Rainwater had always conceived of gourds as an excellent adjunct to her basket projects, both in her classes and as a master basket weaver. She first encountered gourds in her grandmother's garden in the 1920s. She made dipper gourds for water and kept her sewing in a large gourd basket.

As Lois worked more with gourds, the shapes began to indicate to her what they might become on their own, with basketry techniques employed separately for coverings. "I find the problem-solving involved in creating my gourd creatures to be the most fascinating part of the process," she says. "These projects begin with an idea that gradually evolves into their own personality. I always respect and honor their uniqueness and the wonderful artistry they inspire."

Elephant, *Lois Rainwater*

BEADWORK

There are several ways to use the gourd as a foundation for beadwork. One way is to cover the gourd completely with beads, using either netting or a peyote stitch.

This type of beading is similar to the technique used by many cultures in southern Africa. Small bottle gourds are covered completely by beads, often with elaborate colored designs. Gourds such as these may have a face and hair to resemble dolls, and are given to young girls during their initiation period. They frequently have straps attached so that the dolls can be worn around the neck or waist.

A completely different technique requires first putting a foundation over the surface of the gourd to anchor the beads to the surface. These foundations can be composed of many different materials, including wax, glues, and fabrics.

Beaded gourd doll, Ginger Summit

African gourd doll, Dawn Schiller

PROJECT 9

Zulu Beaded Doll, Using Fabric

Dolls like this one are very popular throughout southern Africa, particularly among the Zulu tribes. They are usually created from a firmly stuffed fabric cone or fabric wrapped around a cardboard shape. Wrapping fabric around the body of a gourd can create a similar figure.

1. Choose a gourd for the body and another smaller gourd for the head.

2. Wrap both the body and the head with black fabric, and secure the fabric in place by either stitching or using staples.

3. String beads on floss, and anchor them in place at the base of the figure. Wrap the stringed beads around the body, and tack them in place with a separate needle and thread.

4. Hair was created by pinning stacks of beads onto the head. After the features were stitched in place, the head was stitched and glued onto the body.

Beaded Bottle Gourd, Using Fabric

The Mijikenda people in Kenya make small bottle gourds covered completely by beads, similar to this one. In central Africa, often gourds that are covered completely in beads are first covered entirely with a loose-weave fabric, as done here and in the project described at left.

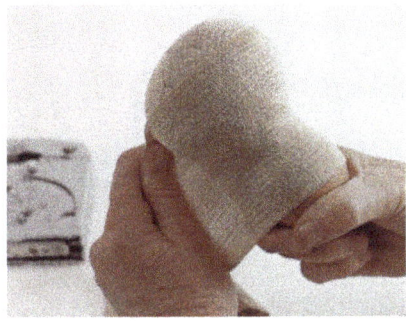

1. Because of the irregular shape of the bottle gourd, an elasticized ace bandage was used instead of regular fabric. The elastic was better able to conform to the shape of the gourd.

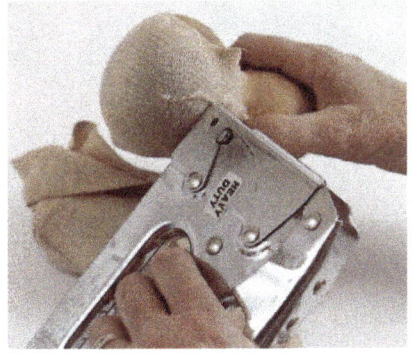

2. A staple gun secures the edges in place.

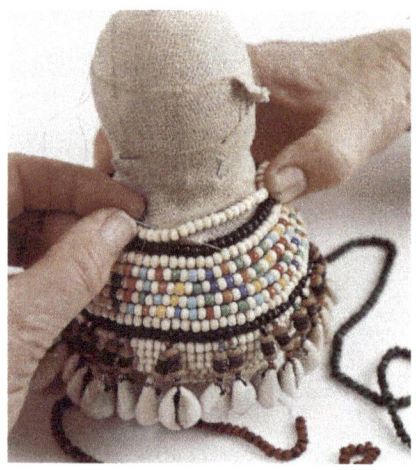

3. Strings of beads are stitched to the fabric, cinching tight to conform to the shape of the gourd.

4. After covering the entire gourd in beads, rub a layer of tar over the surface to fill in the spaces between the beads and help secure them to the fabric.

Fabric is not the only foundation that can be used to anchor beads. The Huichol Indians in Mexico are noted for intricate beaded designs created by pressing individual beads into a combination of wax and pitch. Commercial products are now available for the craftsperson to duplicate this technique on gourds. (See "Beadswax" on page 145.)

Wind, Burst, Fire, *beaded in Huichol style, Dawn Schiller*

Beaded Gourd, Using Tar

A technique similar to that of the Huichol people of North America is also used throughout sub-Saharan Africa, where beads are pressed into a thin layer of pitch. Usually the beads are strung on a thread that helps to anchor them in place so that individual beads cannot be dislodged.

Instead of using pitch, a thick coating of roofing tar is a good substitute. It remains flexible for many hours, but it will dry eventually and hold the beads securely in place.

1. Smear a thin layer of roofing tar on the base of a gourd.

2. Press the end of a string of beads into the tar.

3. Press the beads firmly into place. Cover them with a piece of plastic wrap to control them in the tar. Continue until the gourd is covered completely with beads. To create designs, thread only a few beads at a time and press into place. This will allow you to determine the correct color sequence that is necessary to maintain a design over the curved surface of the gourd. After the entire gourd is covered with beads, wrap in plastic wrap and press the beads into the tar.

4. Clean off the excess tar with paint thinner and allow it to dry.

Finished tar-beaded gourd doll.

CHAPTER 8

Cut & Carved Gourd Dolls

The gourd's unique characteristic is that it is a readymade woodlike sphere right from nature with many advantages for the craftsperson over wood itself. Most important, of course, is that the shapes of gourds are highly individual, stimulating each artist's imagination and creativity. Another advantage is the soft density of the gourd shell compared with most woods. The shells can be cut and carved with relative ease using hand and hobby tools. Because gourds vary greatly in the thickness and density of the shell, many different techniques can be used to create special effects on the shells.

USING CUT SHELLS

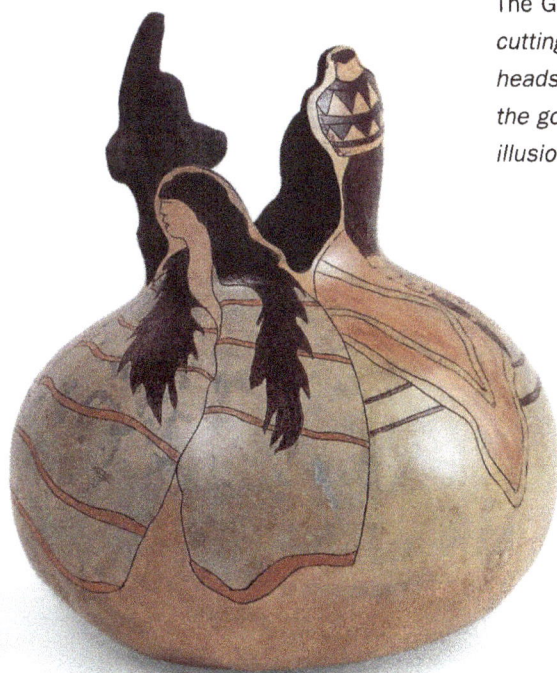

The Gathering, *Ray Baldonado.* By cutting the silhoutte of women's heads around the upper portion of the gourd, the artist creates the illusion of women sitting in a circle.

Nancy Bevans

Nancy Bevans enjoys everything from paints to stone to clay. Gourds fit in naturally with her creative projects. For her, the blemishes and patterns on the gourd contribute to the expression and overall design of the project. Nancy never throws anything away—neither trinkets nor gourd scraps. "You never know when something will be just the right finishing touch for some character," she says. "Gourds are quite miraculous on their own, so to cover them up or disguise their shape would be unthinkable."

Statue of Liberty, *Nancy Bevans.* The gourd's upper portion is cut so as to create a separate piece, which can be turned around, or inverted, to fit into the gourd, becoming a face with a headdress to complement the gourd body.

Mary Pat Smith

About five years ago, a friend invited the artist Mary Pat Smith to a gourd show. Soon after that, she purchased a book to learn more. With the book came seeds, which she planted in her garden. "I harvested a bountiful crop of gourds," she says. "That was the beginning. Now I try to grow most of my own gourds, but buy some at shows and gourd farms."

Gourds have introduced a whole new avenue of artistic expression and experiments. "Anything natural that cannot be reproduced by man or machine has always left me with a sense of amazement," she says. "However, gourds are not only beautiful in their natural state,

Santa Claus, *Mary Pat Smith*. This wonderful Old-World Santa was created from a single gourd that is embellished with carved and shaped pieces from different gourds. The eyebrows, mustache, and beard are composed of many shaped pieces, which are glued in place. The tree is a composite of several sections glued on a single rod and then secured in Santa's hand. The message on the banner was cut out of the gourd shell and illuminated by a small light inserted through an opening in the base of the gourd.

but seem to invite you to explore their possibilities. It is hard not to feel the sacredness of a gourd when you have grown it yourself. Its mystical qualities begin in the seed I have planted, not knowing what the outcome will be."

Mary Pat, who collects and makes Santas, now shapes them from gourds. She describes her process in making this figure: "I first spent hours with pencil and eraser, trying to find the right balance and design. Most of the time, I like as much pure gourd as possible with only a few added embellishments. Working with various paints and dyes, using techniques such as pyrography and carving, and using pieces of gourds become important in providing texture and dimension to the design. The use of gourds for his bag and toys made sense and was a challenge. Whole gourds and parts of gourds were transformed to become part of the whole project."

CARVING

A popular carving technique is to use a rotary power carving tool to remove portions of the background around a wood-burned design. This provides a dramatic contrast both in shading and in surface texture.

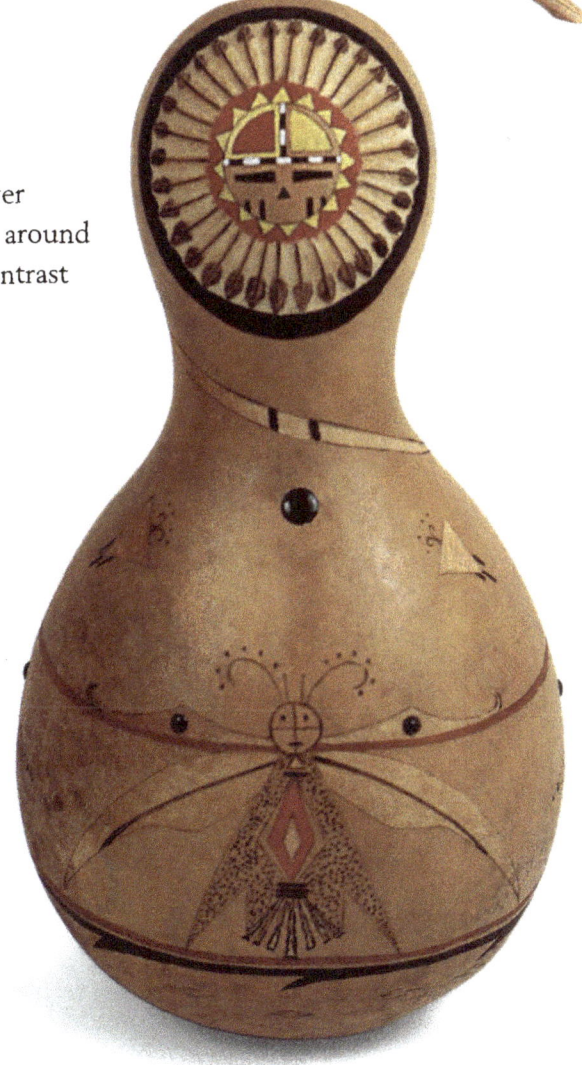

Sun Bottle, *Robert Fox*. *The face mask on this figure was first wood-burned and stained; then the background areas around the feathers were carved away to create depth as well as contrast.*

Sue Jordan

Sue Jordan worked in the corporate world of the East Coast, and she never had time to develop her own artistic side. After moving to New Mexico in the 1990s, she began to explore new talents and interests. Through classes, she has tried many different art projects, but gourd dolls remain a favorite. "I draw on inspiration from the natural colors and patterns of the high desert and the confluence of cultures that makes New Mexico unique," she says.

Corn Maiden, *Sue Jordan*. Most of the maiden's body and the corn in her basket were first dyed and then carved to resemble ears of corn. In addition, the face and front of the body were carved to provide color and surface contrast. The ears of corn in her basket are topped with dried cornhusk.

PROJECT 12

Spirit of Spring

Frequently the spirit within the gourd expresses itself through the curvature and simple elegance of the shell. Nothing needs to be added to the gourd to fulfill this image. Carving simply reveals the spirit that was already there, as with this serene *Spirit of Spring*.

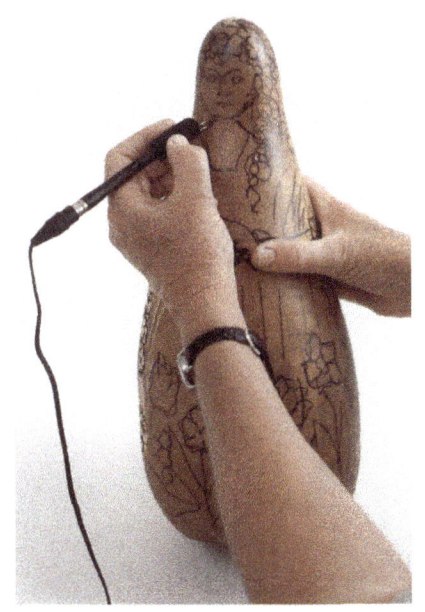

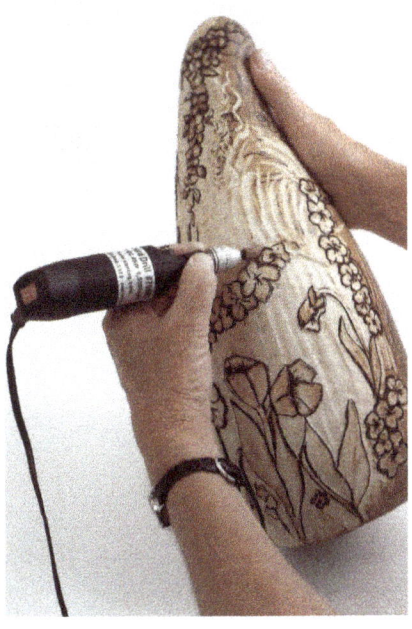

1. Draw the design on the gourd, and wood-burn. This helps create a guide for the carving tool.

GOURD TIP
When considering a project involving sculptural carving, such as this one, use a very thick gourd with an even surface.

2. Use rotary tools to carve around the features and create texture on all surfaces. A combination of bits and sanding tips allows the artist to create many different textures and surfaces. If the carving is particularly deep, it's helpful to insert a hand into the gourd to feel the vibrations of the carving tool. (But be safe. Don't put your directly hand in front of the tool.) If by accident the tool does drill completely through the gourd shell, putty made of white glue mixed with gourd dust can mend the hole with an almost invisible plug.

3. When the carving is completed, a wood burner can be used to highlight parts of the design. Then color the carving with wood dyes and stains, and finish it with an acrylic sealer.

Here is the finished Spirit of Spring.

PROJECT 13

Spirit of Summer

The *Spirit of Summer* needed to burst the bounds of a single gourd shell to be surrounded by the bounty of the harvest of a Mexican summer. The addition of arms and a basket (made of a gourd shell) allowed her to grasp the luxuriance of the season.

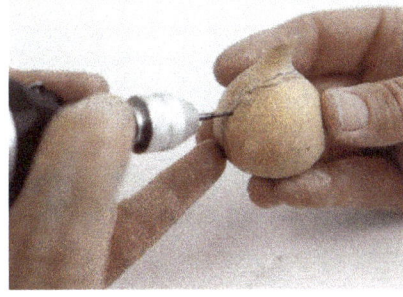

1. Use a small saw or cutting bit on the high-speed drill to cut out a hand shape from a small jewelry gourd.

2. Use a sanding drum or cap to shape the fingers and thumb of the hand.

The completed Spirit of Summer *project expresses the bounty of sunny Mexico.*

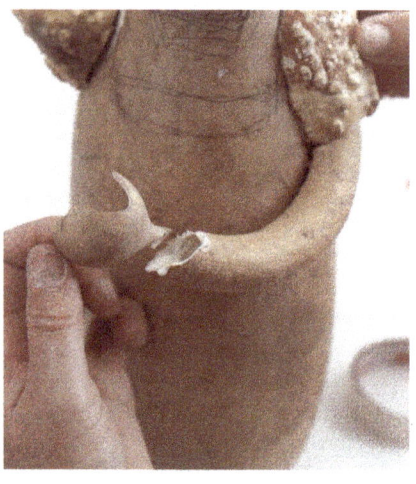

3. Attach the hand with glue to the arm, made from the handle of a dipper gourd.

4. Use masking tape to hold the join together until the glue sets.

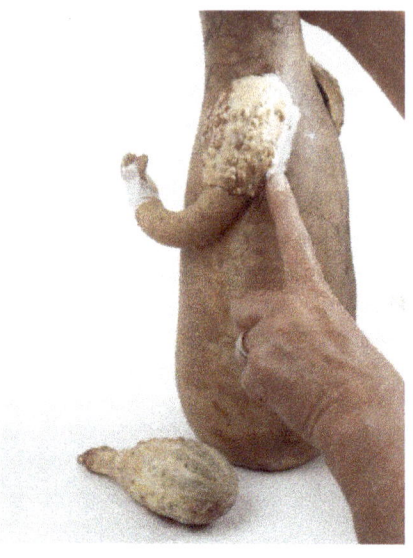

5. With air-drying modeling clay, cover the seams where several gourd pieces have been used to create the arms and shoulders of the figure.

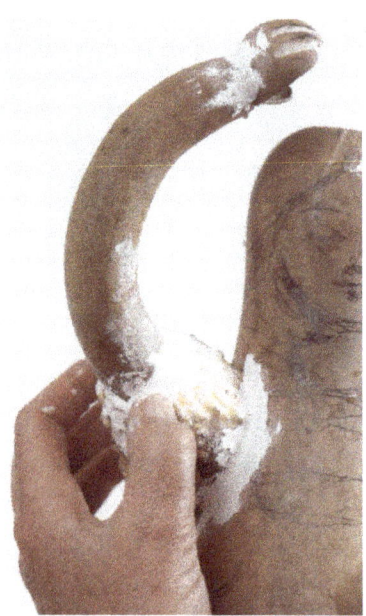

6 and **7.** Moisten your fingers with water to smooth out the modeling clay while it is still pliable. The work you do now will keep you from having to sand the seams later.

8. For the grapes in the bowl of fruit, cut a section from a warty gourd.

PROJECT 14

Autumn Spirit in the Tree

This project is composed completely of gourd pieces and reflects the changing and aging season through the *Autumn Spirit in the Tree*. The snake gourd used for the tree trunk has a very thin shell, so a face carved from a thick gourd piece was added to give features to this tree.

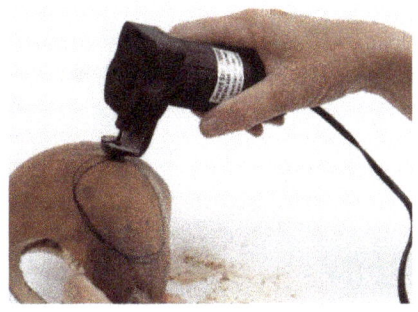

1. With a Gourd Saw, cut out a face-shaped oval from a scrap gourd.

2. After drawing the main parts of the face, use a miniature Gourd Drill with an engraving bit (ball, inverted cone) to carve detail into the face.

Here is the completed Autumn Spirit in the Tree.

4. Delaminate pieces of bark of the paper malaluca tree. (You could also use birch bark or eucalyptus bark, etc).

3. Here is the tree trunk, made from a section of snake gourd, with the gourd face attached. The maranka gourd in the foreground will be cut up to make the roots and branches of the tree.

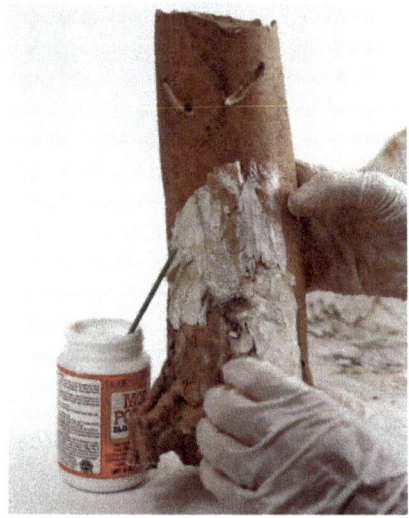

6. Use a Gourd Saw to cut out small leaf-shaped pieces of gourd.

7. Use the sanding cap on a Gourd Drill to smooth the underside of the gourd leaves and add shape to them.

5. Use Mod Podge or a similar product to decoupage the pieces of bark to the section of snake gourd.

8. With a wood-burning tool, darken the edges of the leaves and add detail to the veins on the tops of the leaves.

9. A scattering of gourd leaves can be wired together for stringing on the "tree."

Here is the back of the completed Autumn Spirit in the Tree.

PROJECT 15

Spirit of Winter

This *Spirit of Winter* was constructed from one gourd with several pieces added. The face was carved from a thick gourd scrap, similar to the face in *Autumn Spirit in the Tree*, and glued into place. The arms are made of pieces of dipper gourd glued into place, and the hands are carved from small ornamental gourds. To convey the drapes of heavy cloth, the entire gourd was draped with plaster cloth, similar to that used for making casts. While wet, it can be cut and smoothed to conform to the different shapes of the gourd. Strips of loofa gourd create a furlike trim for the hood.

Here is the completed Spirit of Winter.

The Green Man: Origins and Symbolism

The image of the Green Man, or a face peering through leaves or foliage, is a haunting one in churches and cathedrals throughout Europe and the British Isles. It is difficult to identify where this image comes from, because it is found in early Greek and Roman architecture and friezes and throughout Mesopotamia. When Rome penetrated Europe, this image was no doubt spread to the new territories and became associated with many different gods and religious practices. The most common interpretation of these early images is that they were an effort to place a face on nature, to represent some of the mysterious seasonal changes that were such a fundamental part of the daily lives of the people.

The early church adopted and adapted these images and gave them a distinct interpretation. While many early pagan images are quite benevolent or mischievous, the images often found in sixth century churches are dark and brooding or sinister. The Green Man gradually became associated with the demon, and in the ninth century the "spirit of nature" became associated with the "sins of nature." Thus, the carvings in medieval churches often are full of horror and savage expressions. By the fifteenth and sixteenth centuries, the Green Man was assigned a dual role, part goblin and part godlike, and eventually took on the more benign concept of "springtime of grace," or a coming to terms with nature.

Common to all images throughout this turbulent history is a foliated head or a mask surrounded by leaves. Usually a penetrating stare (or glare) peers out from leaves, often acanthus, but also oak, grape, and other vines. While some faces are exposed completely, with leaves or vines surrounding the features, others have vines exuding from the nostrils and mouth. When the Green Man was depicted as a demon, the tongue protruded and many faces even had fangs—a fearsome view of nature at its most harsh.

Today, interest in the Green Man has surged as people are reconnecting with the natural world and festivals are held to celebrate the seasons. The image reappears in songs, myths, and decorative elements that grace our lives, a reminder of our role as stewards of the earth.

PROJECT 16

Green Man

With four faces representing the seasons, around the sides of a thick canteen gourd, this project is a variation of the more traditional Green Man designs. For the sake of simplicity, however, the instructions that follow are for only one face. You can make the Green Man either way, with four faces or just one. Two different primary techniques are shown here, first carving and then decoupage. The instructions for applying decoupage are specifically for creating a piece with one face.

Green Man, Carving Technique

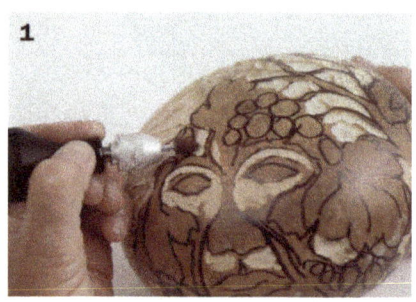
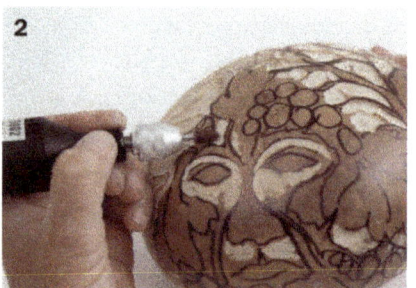

1. Mark the outline of the design on the gourd and use coarse sanding tips to remove the tough outer layer of shell.

2, 3, and **4.** Use a variety of engraving bits (ball tip, inverted cone, cylinder), as needed, to remove portions of the shell and add texture to the surfaces.

Green Man, Decoupage Technique

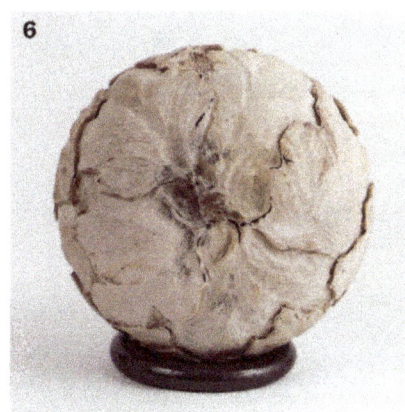

5 and **6.** After the gourd is carved completely, protect the surface with a wood sealer.

7. Apply leather dyes and stains to create a weathered and shaded effect.

GOURD TIP
If you want the leaves to remain green and flexible, use florist-prepared (freeze-dried, PEG-impregnated) leaves and ferns.

134 CUT & CARVED DOLLS

1. In this second Green Man, only facial features are carved into the gourd. Paint decoupage glue on the rest of the surface and layer small freshly dried oak leaves in place on the back of the gourd.

2 and **3.** Use plastic wrap to hold the leaves in place while you repeat the process on the front of the gourd.

4. Check and make sure all leaves are glued down. Use your brush to add glue where needed.

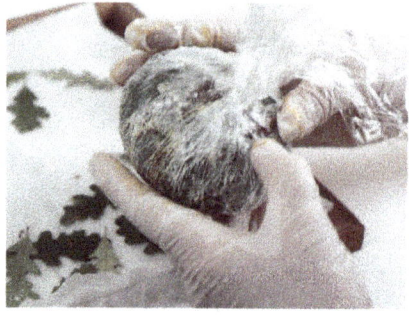

5. When all the leaves are in place, wrap the entire gourd with plastic wrap and "massage" the surface to remove any air bubbles and to make sure that the leaves conform completely to the gourd's surface.

6. After they're dry, lightly gild the leaves with a gold powder to enhance the leaf veins. Here is the finished Green Man, using the decopage technique.

CHAPTER NINE

Dolls with Hidden Treasures & Nesting Dolls

CREATING CAVITIES

Dolls have served many functions in society through the ages. One feature of many figurines is having a space within either the head or the body, and this cavity has been used in unusual and exotic ways.

In many cultures in Africa, where dolls were often the property of shamans or healers, a space was frequently carved in the body to hold sacred materials: powders with special properties, remnants of deceased ancestors, or powerful totems to ward off evil spirits. In Europe, courtly attendants used these spaces to hide forbidden messages, which could then be passed to other members of court in secret. The matryoshka doll in Russia, instead of holding similar shaped dolls in graduated sizes, frequently held treats or novelty gifts for the lucky recipient. In America, settlers and pioneers used dolls for hiding money or other family treasures in case their homes were raided.

Gourds provide a very attractive way to pass on this tradition, because they are naturally hollow. Entrances can be made in the body of the gourd, which can then be left open or secured, and contain a little treasure.

Jo Ann Vanderheite

Art teacher Jo Ann Vanderheite worked with a wide variety of materials. Yet gourds presented a fresh and challenging art form that allowed her to apply all her skills. Like other gourd artists, Jo Ann says the gourds she chooses "seem to call to me from the gourd pile. There is definitely a communication between us."

For her gourd-doll container, she "tried to keep the design simple, because the shape of the gourd was so demanding. When I first found it sitting by itself near a pile of other gourds, it spoke very clearly of human qualities. I wanted to create a minimal face in the style of early American folk art. For useful purposes, I divided the gourd into two parts at the neckline to serve as a container without spoiling the flow of the design."

Gourd-doll container, Jo Ann Vanderheite

A Resting Place, *Pat Boyd*

CREATING CAVITIES **137**

Ratna Djuhadi ("Ardee")

Ardee lives in Hawaii, which has a rich tradition of arts and crafts. She draws on images from her own experience, using primarily natural materials. About decorating gourds, Ardee says, "It is too easy to ruin a beautiful natural gourd so that it loses its identity."

Mother and Child, *Ratna Djuhadi ("Ardee")*

African Lady, *Fonda Haddad*. African Lady *represents the spirit of African craftswomen. Made of two gourds, painted black all over, the lady contains a center of basketry reed, which forms her upper body. The reed is twined and covered with beading and a pendant necklace. Her head, made from the second gourd, is adorned with loop earrings and a yarn topknot and can be removed.*

Lynette Dawson

Lynette Dawson was introduced to gourds many years ago when a friend was selling ornamental gourds, and she has been working with them ever since. Although she lives in the backwoods of Michigan, she has accumulated hundreds of gourds from visiting friends and gourd farms. When she selects a gourd, with an idea for a project, the gourd often leads her in a different direction that's usually better than her original idea, she says. For each doll type that Lynette creates, she researches the culture it represents to avoid offending any group that may have inspired her piece.

Bounty, *figure with open shelves, Lynette Dawson*

Message Doll, *Lynette Dawson. Message paper wrapped around the doll becomes her clothing.*

Cathy Burton

Cathy Burton sees her gourd constructions as sculpture and interprets myths and fables through her art. Working in arts education in a museum setting, she encounters artists and traditions from the past as well as the present. "I believe what makes us human is the ability to create," she says, "and the world is a better place when we can find a way to communicate through the arts. The surface of the gourd seems to invite the creative spirit, rather than resist certain techniques or styles. The wonderful thing about gourds is their versatility."

Day of the Dead, #3, *Cathy Burton*

Day of the Dead, #2, *Cathy Burton*

Sprout, *Doris Hensen. Collection of Marcia Oberbreckling.*

140 DOLLS WITH HIDDEN TREASURES & NESTING DOLLS

Peruvian doll, interior. Collection of Gertrude Turner.

Peruvian doll. Collection of Gertrude Turner.

PROJECT 17

Mother Goose

Mother Goose was made to provide a home for the many puppets created for this book. It was inspired by a large Indonesian bottle-gourd figure that resembled a protective mother bird, and parts of other gourds were added to complete the image. The beak was carved from a separate gourd and glued into place. The feet are cut from scraps of a Maranka gourd, which has ribbed texture suggesting the webbed feet. Glasses created out of wire wrapped with black tape surround eyes of onyx. Protective wings, allowing many small puppets to nestle together when not in use, cover the large hole in the side. See step directions on page 142.

NESTING

Sets of nesting dolls can be made in a variety of shapes and styles. The challenge is to find graduated sizes of gourds with similar shapes that can fit easily inside each other. The round-ball or egg shape may be the simplest with which to start.

1. Position the wing, and hold it in place with masking tape and support.

2. Glue the denim fabric piece to help support the weight of the wing.

3. Stitch through the fabric and gourd wing to anchor the attachment securely.

Matryoshka Dolls

Although most often associated with Russian folk art, the nesting doll actually originated in Japan, with sets of round nesting dolls representing the Buddhist sage Fukuruma. One of these sets was taken to Russia in the late nineteenth century, and artists there re-created it as the matryoshka doll that is so popular today. The name *matryoshka* most likely comes from the Russian word *mat*, for mother, combined with the suffix *oshka*, to mean "little mother."

The doll is usually made of linden wood, which is easy to carve on a lathe. The popularity of this type of doll had declined, but because of the current renaissance in preserving traditional Russian cultural objects, small workshops throughout the country now produce them. The early doll sets were made in rounded shapes and usually depicted young girls dressed in traditional clothing decorated with flowers. Today, the nesting dolls are made in various shapes and convey a range of images. Some are religious or political or represent literary figures or architectural landmarks. The sets can contain anywhere from three or four to as many as thirty pieces. Another variation consists of a single large figure that contains many small, related objects or hidden treasures, which themselves do not open.

PROJECT 18

Matryoshka Set

This set of nesting dolls is based on the typical Russian matryoshka doll.

1. First find a graduated series of gourds that will fit inside each other when cut in half. After this series was started, I found an additional gourd to fill the gap between the second and third gourds, making a complete set of eight gourds.

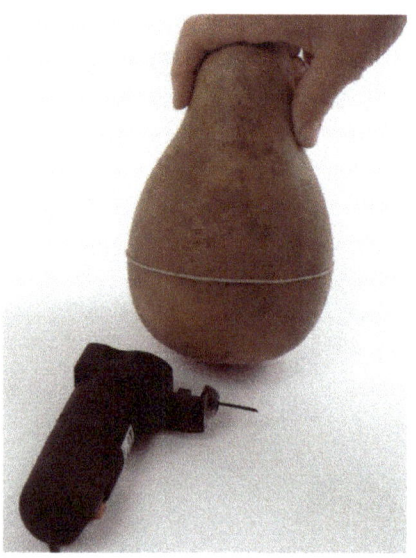

2. Find the widest point of the "belly" of the gourds, and cut the gourd horizontally. Clean the interior, and test to make sure that the gourds "nest." It may be necessary to sand some of the interior shell in the gourds, so be careful not to penetrate the shell. If the shell becomes thin, you can reinforce it by gluing gauze tape to the inside.

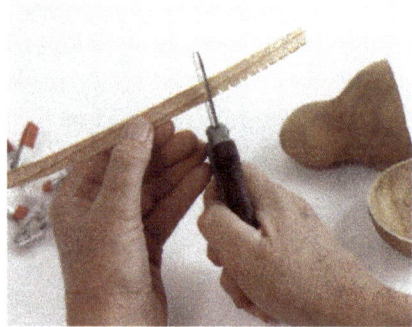

3. Cut a ¾-inch (2-cm) flat reed to fit the circumference of each gourd, and soak for several minutes until it becomes flexible. Cut wedges from one edge of the reed, to allow for the curvature of the inside of the gourd.

4. With a strong wood glue, secure the reed in place with small clamps or clothespins until completely dry.

5. The gourd is now ready for decorating. In this example, I first painted the face with a neutral-colored paint and the belly of the gourd with ivory. Then I painted the rest of the gourd with barn-red acrylic paint.

6. When the paint is completely dry, paint a border of matching gloss enamel around the face and belly areas.

7. Fill in the features and belly area with acrylic designs appropriate to this style of doll. To add detail along the border, use gold-paint pens.

DECORATIVE TECHNIQUES

What follows are additional techniques that you can use to decorate matryoshka dolls. By keeping the shape constant, it is interesting to see the various effects that can be achieved by the different craft materials used to decorate gourds. Of course, you can apply these techniques to other figures besides matryoshka dolls.

Painting

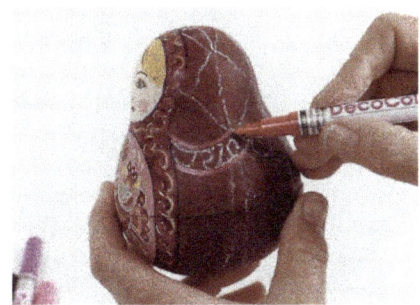

1. Start by covering the gourd with a base of acrylic paints, as with the gourds in the set described earlier.

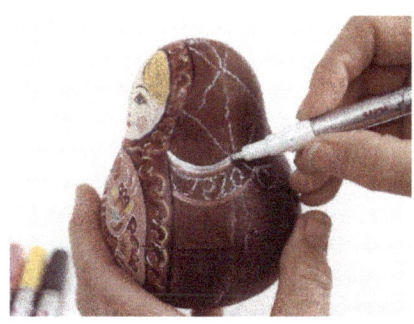

2. In this case, all further decoration is made using enamel-paint pens, readily available either separately or in sets of eight or twelve colors.

Beadswax

1. Sand down the belly of the gourd using a rotary sander, approximately 1/8 inch (3 mm). Also gouge out a channel to create a border around the face and the belly of the gourd. Draw a pattern on the sanded surfaces, which is then covered with a thin layer of combined beeswax and pitch. Using a special tool similar to an awl fitted with a stopper, embed individual beads into the wax following the pattern.

2. To fill in the channels around the face and belly, press beads strung on floss into the spaces. Drill additional design elements of small flowers into the border area and fill them with matching beads. Wood-burn a face to complete the doll.

Carving

1. First, wood-burn a design onto the gourd, to provide a pattern and guide for the hobby rotary tool. Dye the gourd medium brown, except for the face. Remove the background surrounding the pattern in the belly of the gourd to provide a nice contrast with the floral design.

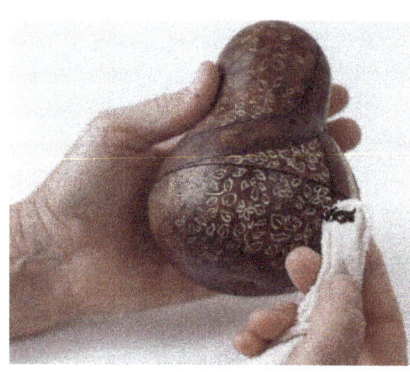

2. Carve a smaller floral pattern into the shawl and dress.

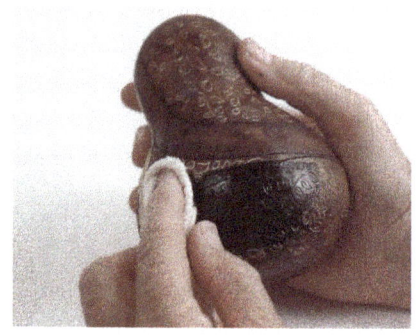

3. Rub black paint into the design.

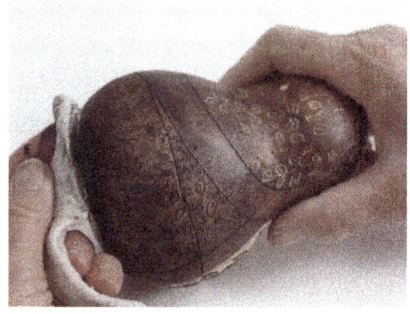

4. Then quickly wipe off the black paint, leaving a subtle dark "brocade" effect. Carve matching floral patterns into the border area surrounding the face and belly.

5. The finished gourd demonstrates three different effects that can be achieved by carving.

Inlay with Inlace Resin

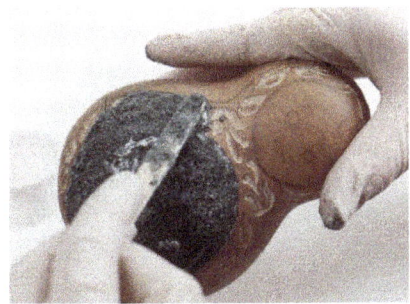

1. After drawing the general design on the gourd, use a rotary carver to remove approximately ¼ inch (6 mm) of the surface of the gourd in both the belly area and other designs to be filled in with the inlay. Mix the inlay according to directions, and smooth over the carved surfaces.

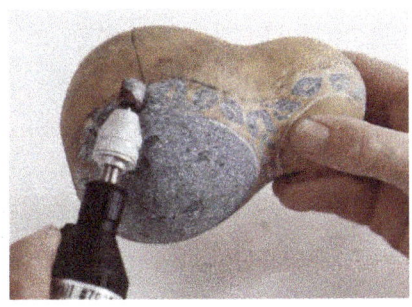

2. When the inlay is completely dry, use the sanding bit on the rotary power tool to smooth the surface. When the surface is smoothed, continue using finer grits until the surface of the inlay is very smooth. Apply a polish to bring out the greatest color.

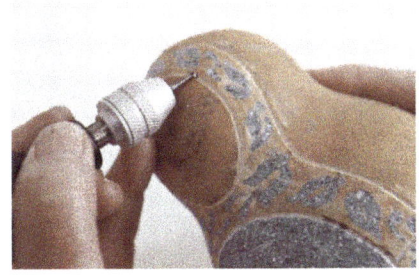

3. Using a rotary power tool, gouge a channel around the face and belly, creating a border.

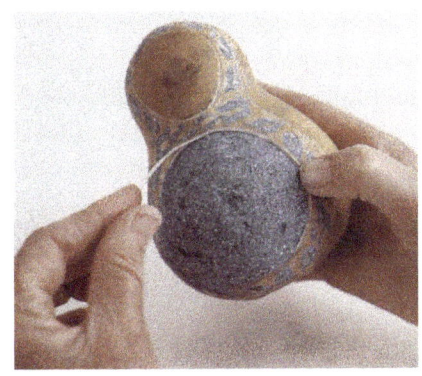

4. Glue ½ round silver wire into the channels.

5. Lightly sketch a design on the surface of the inlay. Use a small engraving bit on the rotary power tool to carve away the background surrounding the design. This creates a contrast between the polished surface of the design and the carved background.

6. Finished set of dolls showing various embellishment techniques, including beadswax, inlay, wood-burning, carving, netting, and painting.

Netted matryoshka doll, Ginger Summit. The knotless netting was created on the gourd. Upholstery gimp was glued over the edging and then embellished with beads.

CHAPTER TEN
Weighted Dolls

KEEPING DOLLS UPRIGHT

To our surprise, a novel figure, the "weighted doll," is found in many places around the world. Typically, it is created of a material that has a rounded bottom, making it difficult to stay in an upright position. During construction, a weight is secured to the bottom of the form, so that even if tipped, it will return to the upright position.

These figures are sometimes referred to as "tumbler dolls" or "roly-poly dolls." Figures that have this feature may be associated with a myth or a moral lesson—even when distracted or knocked off balance, the spirit will return to the original goal, signifying loyalty, fidelity, or uprightness.

Weighted doll, with button eyes, cloth, and beads, Ginger Summit, is similar to those given to young girls in West Africa.

DARUMA DOLLS, AFRICAN INITIATION DOLLS & OTHER DOLLS

Daruma Dolls

A very popular symbol of good luck in Japan is the round, eyeless daruma doll. These dolls come in many shapes and sizes, but they're usually made of papier-mâché, painted bright red, and many have a bold eyeless face. Although some are made with a base, more often they are created as tumbler dolls.

The origin of this image is the grand patriarch of Zen Buddhism in China. He originally came from India in the fifth or sixth century and traveled north and east to China. One of the legends surrounding this sage is that in his search for enlightenment he sat facing a wall for seven years without moving. During this time, his arms and legs atrophied and fell off. According to another legend, at one point during meditation he dozed off and then ordered that his eyelids be cut off so that his vision would not be blocked.

During New Years' celebrations, daruma dolls are given as gifts for good luck. When the recipients make a wish or a resolution for the coming year, they paint in one eye. When that wish comes true, the second eye is filled in. In many temples in Japan, the old daruma dolls are burned to make way for the New Year and new aspirations.

Weighted doll, with painted yellow polka-dot blouse, Christi Tsai

PROJECT 19

Weighted Daruma Doll

In Japan, the popular daruma figure often is represented as a weighted tumbler doll, conveying the message that even when serious monks are knocked about or distracted, they return to their upright, meditating pose.

1. Cut the bottom out of a small egg-shaped gourd.

2. Glue on some weights, such as stones (here, heavy washers and bolts are used).

3. When the glue has dried completely, reattach the bottom of the gourd to the body. Reinforce the seam with strips of lightweight gauze. The edges can be sanded lightly or covered with a thin layer of clay.

4. Add the distinctive daruma facial features, with a rim of clay surrounding the face.

5. Smooth the rim of clay around the edges to blend with the gourd surface.

6. Paint the gourd with acrylic paints in a style to resemble this popular figure. The eyes are intentionally left white. The owner can then fill in one eye when he or she has made a wish or a New Year's resolution. If the wish is fulfilled, the second eye is colored in.

Weighted doll, with painted red Mandarin top, Christi Tsai

Humpty-Dumpty, Ginger Summit

African Initiation Dolls

Throughout western and southern Africa, dolls are given to girls during initiation ceremonies. One style, which is most prevalent in southern Africa, is weighted and composed of two rounded gourds attached at the middle. These dolls were wrapped with various materials, including strings of beads, cloth, leather, and plant fiber. Some were given rudimentary features made of beads or shells, but they usually remain faceless.

While they are often described as "fertility dolls," given to young girls during their initiation ceremonies, at least one form of the figure is associated with implements given to young boys during their initiation. They may have been filled with special potions or materials that promise strength and protection. These figures have also been found in the collections of shamans and healers in many villages throughout southern Africa.

Weighted doll, with beads around the neck, Ginger Summit

PROJECT 20

African Weighted Doll

This project was inspired by the weighted initiation dolls of southern Africa, which generally have no facial features and are wrapped with strings or beads and other materials.

1. Select two small bottle gourds with rounded bottoms and with a similar diameter in the neck portion. Cut off the end of one gourd and pour in some weights, such as BBs. Sand, plaster, or gravel would also be suitable.

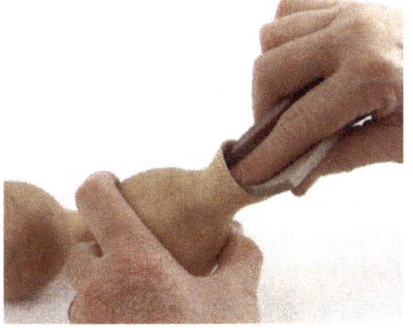

3. Sand the edges of the opening of the gourd.

2. Add glue, and let it dry completely.

4. Glue in the second gourd.

5. Wrap the center portion of the figure with cloth, rope, or beads.

CHAPTER ELEVEN

Instruments

SACRED IMAGES

Music has long been considered a very important part of the sacred rituals and ceremonies throughout the world. Music is often felt to be a vital link in the communication between the visible and invisible worlds, a special way to connect with the spiritual forces that affect daily life. The instruments themselves became objects of significance and often were carved from gourds with images both to inspire the musician and to reflect the ethereal nature of the sounds produced. The carved drums found in Africa are perhaps the most vivid examples of this.

Many small stringed instruments similar to the hunter's harp are found throughout West Africa. Historically, they were played in ceremonies preceding a hunt, calling on the spirits to guide the hunters to success on their search for food. Today, these instruments are played in festivals, but still retain the images that recall spiritual connections.

Contemporary lute from Kenya

HUNTER'S HARP, RATTLES & OTHER INSTRUMENTS

Human images are found adorning many different types of instruments from around the world. The humanlike features often served to add a personal connection between the musicians and the spirits they invoked.

Rattle, Christi Tsai

Hunter's harp from Kenya

156 INSTRUMENTS

Gourd trumpet, Kemper Stone

Peruvian guiro (rasp)

Rain stick, Ginger Summit

Kachina rattle, Robert Rivera.
Collection of Sher Elliott-Widess.

Warrior Mouse rattle, Lyle Lomayma

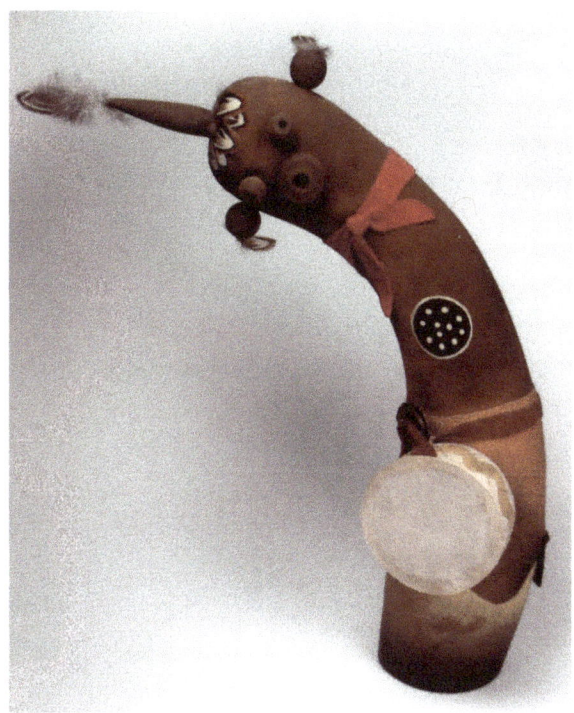

Mud Man rattle, Bonnie Gibson

In Africa, the cult of ancestors holds important religious significance. Crafters, because the musical instrument is an extension of the performer's soul, go out of their way to imbue the instrument's shape with human qualities. The head, as source of sound and speech, tends to be the most frequently fashioned part of the human figure. Crafters also draw on sound-producing animal figures, such as birds. Music and dance may be accompanied only by decorated instruments. The decoration brings high esteem to the instrument through ownership or the accomplished craftsman. Often the instrument itself is shaped like a human torso to which the artist adds a carved head and maybe appendages to complete the figure.

Kalimba from the Dan Tribe, Ivory Coast

Contemporary rattle from the Kamba tribe, Kenya

CHAPTER TWELVE
Puppets

There is a basic difference between puppets and many of the dolls and spirit figures considered thus far. The original function of dolls and figures in society was as a vehicle for healing or instruction or as a means to link the visible and invisible worlds. When dolls were made specifically for children or young people, they were used as tools to teach appropriate roles that the child would later assume in adult life. For the most part, these dolls occupied an imaginary world of the owner. In contrast, puppets were intended to educate or create an imaginary world for an audience.

Stick puppet, Christi Tsai

STICK PUPPETS

A simple style of puppet found around the world is the stick, or rod, puppet. It consists of a simple head on a stick, which is bobbed about to create a character, or perhaps just placed in a vase or on a stand to provide a small decorative accent. If used as a puppet, it may have a simple costume. The more elaborate variation has hands controlled by separate rods.

There are several ways to make a stick puppet with a gourd. Perhaps the easiest is to simply paint a face on a small gourd and secure it to the end of a rod. No costuming is required, although a collar may help to disguise the seam.

A dipper gourd provides a natural stick puppet. All you need to do is make a face on the bulb of the gourd and embellish it with hair or other ornamentation. If you wish to add arms, make a simple cloth form similar to a hand puppet. These simple puppets can be given an additional dimension by adding flexible arms, which are controlled by two rods, manipulated by the puppeteer's other hand.

Stick puppet, Emiko Matsutsuyu

PROJECT 21

Fairy Godmother Stick Puppet

The Fairy Godmother is shown here, but you can use these instructions to create any stick puppet you want to make. The puppet is simple—basically consisting of a dipper gourd and cloth arms, with hands controlled by rods.

1. Sand a dipper gourd, and then give it a face with marking pens.

2. Add uncombed fleece for hair.

3. Dress the puppet, adding two arms of cloth. Glue rods to each hand.

Here are Cinderella, the Prince, and the Fairy Godmother in a "pumpkin" (gourd) carriage with gourd wheels.

POP-UP PUPPETS

This variation of a stick puppet includes a cone, into which the puppet head and body can disappear.

Pop-up puppet, Sue Westhues

PROJECT 22

Daybreak Pop-Up Puppet

While normally pop-up puppets are small and playful, the concept holds great potential for expressing many other ideas for the gourd artist. The challenge is to find gourds that are compatible in size and shape. For this project, a large dipper gourd wanted to become an exotic spirit-of-life force but needed a resting space. The directions below can be applied to any pop-up puppet.

1. Prepare a dipper gourd with clay features.

2. Then you need to find a cone-shaped gourd that will have plenty of room for the gourd as well as the clay face and clothing.

3. Fasten a robe to the neck of the dipper gourd and to the rim of the cone.

Daybreak, *finished gourd*

TOPSY-TURVY PUPPETS

The topsy-turvy doll, with its reversible heads, is considered a traditional American folk doll. It is sometimes called an "upside-down doll," because two (or more) figures are joined at the waist, one of which can be hidden by a skirt or other clothing. The most famous version of this doll is "Topsy and Eva," which is composed of a black girl's face and simple attire on one side and a white girl with a frilly frock on the other. Another popular form consisted of two babies, one sleeping and the other very wide awake. Topsy-turvy dolls were popular throughout the Appalachia region for many years in the nineteenth century.

More recently, these dolls have been made as puppets that combine two or more characters in a folk tale. In the most familiar forms, this type of doll was made with cloth, but it is easily adapted to gourds.

Little Bo-Peep and the Little Lost Sheep *(the same topsy-turvy doll right side up and flipped upside down)*, *Ginger Summit*

PROJECT 23

Night and Day Topsy-Turvy Puppet

These directions can be applied to any topsy-turvy puppet.

1. Find two gourds of approximately the same size. Drill holes in the base of both gourds, and glue them together using a dowel to secure the join.

Night and Day

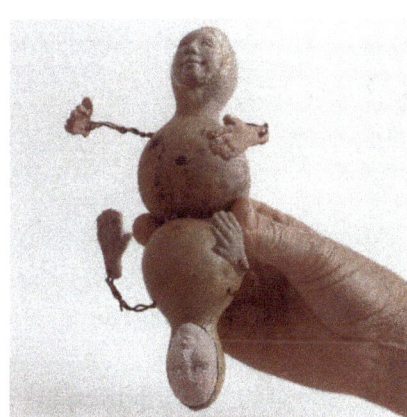
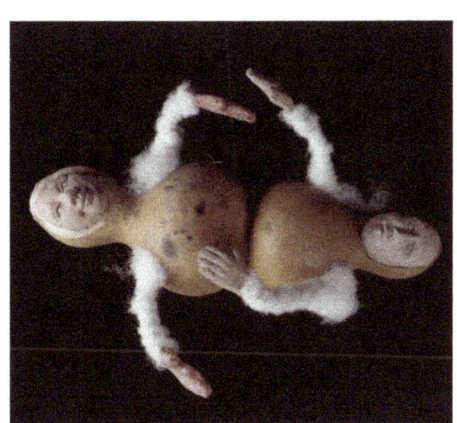

2. Then embellish the heads to create separate personalities. For this puppet, clay faces and wire arms were added. The costuming should consist of skirts or robes that can drape down and hide the opposite face.

Here, Night is holding the moon.

Day holds the gold-leafed sun.

FINGER PUPPETS

A very easy type of puppet to make is the finger puppet. Simply cut a hole in the base of a small gourd, draw on a face, and then slip the puppet onto your finger. It can be "dressed" by cutting a circle of fabric to cover the finger before putting on the head. The gourd heads can be made more decorative with the addition of hair, and more elaborate clothing can be used.

PROJECT 24

The Three Little Pigs and Little Red Riding Hood Finger Puppet

By using a garden glove to cover the hand, several gourds can be attached to the fingers to tell a complete story. The heads can be permanently attached to the glove, or they can be removable simply by making an appropriate-size hole in the base of the gourd.

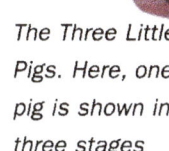

The Three Little Pigs. Here, one pig is shown in three stages

The Wolf and Little Red Riding Hood

HAND PUPPETS

A hand puppet is made much like a finger puppet, only on a slightly larger scale. Select a medium-size gourd, and cut a hole large enough for at least one or perhaps two fingers to fit. Make a costume with arms large enough to accommodate a thumb on one side and remaining fingers on the other. At the neck of the costume, make a "tube" that will either fit into the gourd or around the neck of the gourd, allowing for the costume to be stitched onto the gourd. Embellish with hair, a hat, and other accessories to create a character.

PUZZLE DOLLS & MR. GOURD HEAD

The next two projects are puzzle dolls and Mr. Gourd Head, which is a variation of the popular children's toy, Mr. Potato Head. While not puppets, they have been included here, because, as with puppets, children can play with them.

Both projects take advantage of the spherical, hollow nature of the gourd to make a doll with a feeling of whimsy. As gourds come in such a wide variety of shapes and sizes, simply let your imagination explore all the possibilities.

Two clown hand puppets, Rebecca Black

PROJECT 25

Humpty-Dumpty Puzzle Doll

Although instructions for creating *Humpty-Dumpty* are given here, the basic concept can be applied to any puzzle doll. To make this into a puzzle doll with many pieces so that it can be reassembled, the gourd was cut into several rings that can stack together. The cut lines are irregular so as to allow for a more secure fit between the pieces.

1. This egg-shaped gourd is actually a composite of two gourds. The main portion was a bottle gourd that had been grown on a trellis, so it didn't have a flattened bottom or side. A scrap removed from a second gourd made a perfect top for this project. The two pieces were sanded until they fit to create an egg shape. The resulting egg gourd was then sponged with several coats of white and ivory acrylic to create a surface much like that of an egg. Before being decorated, the gourd was cut with irregular lines into several rings, and the edges were smoothed and painted to match the surface of the gourd. Then a weight was added to the inside of the bottom portion for stability.

2. Modeling clay was added to create the collar and tie. Rope was covered with cloth and then anchored firmly into the appropriate sections of the gourd to create arms and legs. The hands and feet were shaped from mini-gourds.

Here's Humpty-Dumpty *after the fall*.

PROJECT 26

Mr. Gourd Head Puzzle Doll

This simple project has interchangeable parts, as with the commercial Mr. Potato Head. A bottle gourd was inverted, and two feet cut from a single mini-gourd were glued onto the smaller end to provide stability. Arms were cut from sections of a dipper gourd and fitted with hands carved from mini-gourds.

Many different accessories can be created for this little fellow using scraps from other projects. In this case, the ears were cut from gourd scraps and glued in place. All the other facial features are interchangeable, with dowels that fit into holes drilled into the face of the gourd. Use heavy-duty glue to attach short lengths of dowel to the back of each piece. This little project can inspire lots of variations!

Meet Mr. Gourd Head *and a few accessories.*

CHAPTER THIRTEEN
Jewelry & Ornaments

WEARABLE ART

Most gourd crafters soon find themselves surrounded by piles of scraps too precious to throw away. Or small gourds are sometimes overlooked in the search for the perfect gourd for a larger project.

There are many ways to turn these items into wearable art. By wood-burning, painting, adding beads, and using other decorative techniques, small pieces of gourd shell are transformed into figurative finery that can enhance any clothing.

Amulet for the Soul *pin*,
Beverly Shamana

Agate *pin, Beverly Shamana*

Beverly Shamana

"I find that when I work on a gourd, it also works on me. I become a conduit for the expression of the design that is often beyond my rational mind. At some point in the process, I must get out of the way for the essence of the art to come forth.

"When working on a gourd doll, I am open to discovery and risk. I remind myself that giving creative birth means walking two steps into the dark to find the place where ideas come to life. This is a process that I do not take for granted.

"I do feel that the gourd is a humble and powerful part of divine creation."

Geisha *pin, Beverly Shamana*

WEARABLE ART **173**

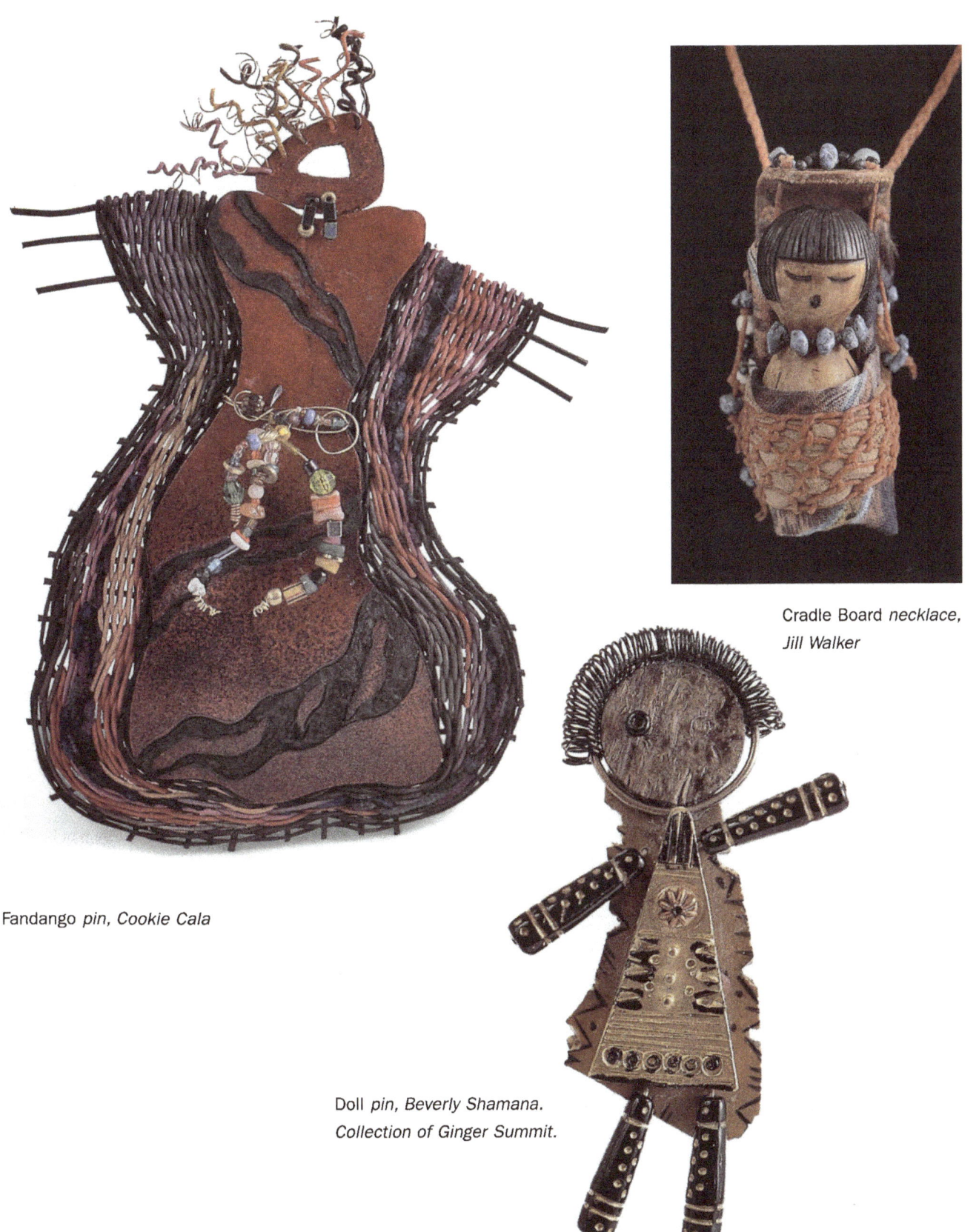

Fandango pin, Cookie Cala

Cradle Board necklace, Jill Walker

Doll pin, Beverly Shamana.
Collection of Ginger Summit.

174 JEWELRY & ORNAMENTS

Wire-Hair Doll *pins*, Linda Noblitt

Nametag *necklace*, Diane Piccola

Mermaid *pins*, Linda Noblitt

DECORATIONS FOR THE HOME   **175**

Medicine Woman *and* Medicine *pins, Tia Flores*

Corn Kachina *necklace, Jill Walker*

Broken Spirits *pin,*
Cookie Cala

Bluebird *pendant,*
Leah Comerford

Tapir *pendant,*
Leah Comerford

176 JEWELRY & ORNAMENTS

DECORATIONS FOR THE HOME

When we think of ornaments, we often think of just the Christmas holiday season, when homes are decorated with an abundance of small ornaments in almost every room. These days, however, ornaments appear at all times of year to witness the changing seasons, the holidays and festivals year-round, or special family occasions. Gourds provide a wonderful medium to help express the richness of family traditions.

Carved-and-burned Santa ornament, Tito Medina

Angel ornament, Jo Cooley

Carved-and-burned owl ornament, Tito Medina

DECORATIONS FOR THE HOME 177

Nun, country girl, and nurse ornaments, CeCe Thomas

Cat ornament, CeCe Thomas

CHAPTER FOURTEEN

Animals

Gourd cat sculpture, Virginia and Wayne Page

While the original intention of this book was to investigate the human figure expressed through gourds, it soon became obvious that the spirit in the gourd can also assume other shapes—of animals and mysterious creatures. Making human and animal figures requires the same skills and imagination, so we have included some examples of animals here for your inspiration.

Paying Tribute to a Master

One of the undisputed masters of this genre was Minnie Black, a gourd artist of unparalleled creativity. In the 1950s, she began growing gourds in her yard in Kentucky after finding some growing wild along her driveway. Once the bounty appeared, her artistic side took over, and she turned them into all kinds of marvelous instruments, animals, and human figures.

She used Sculptamold™ to fill the joins of the multiple gourds she used, but most of the creations are composed simply of gourds, hidden beneath layers of paint. Minnie died in 1996, at the age of ninety-eight. She left a legacy of great spirit, imagination, and the sheer joy of freedom in playing with the gourd.

Dragon, *Minnie Black*.
Collection of Ginger Summit.

PROJECT 27

Moose

This project, focusing on the antlers, was created by gourd artist Jennifer Norpchen.

Here are the two finished moose by Jennifer Norpchen.

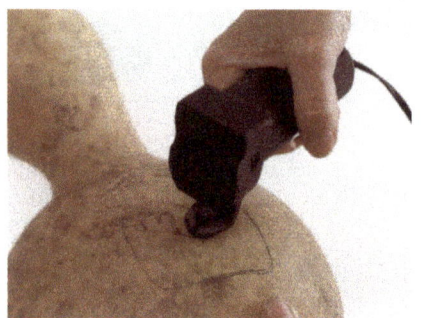

1. To make the moose antlers, Jennifer uses the miniature Gourd Saw to cut out the section after she draws the outline with a pencil.

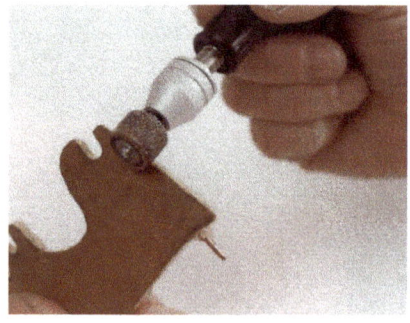

2. She uses the miniature Gourd Drill with a sanding drum to smooth the edges and perfect the shape of the antlers.

3. She places the two antlers on the moose's head to determine the position behind the eye sockets, made from an air-drying modeling clay.

MOOSE   **181**

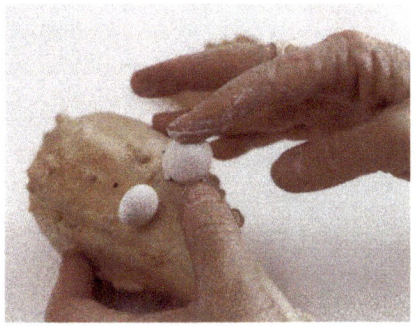

4. With her moistened fingers, she shapes the eye sockets.

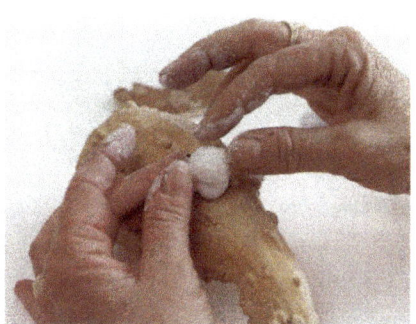

5. You can add more clay if necessary.

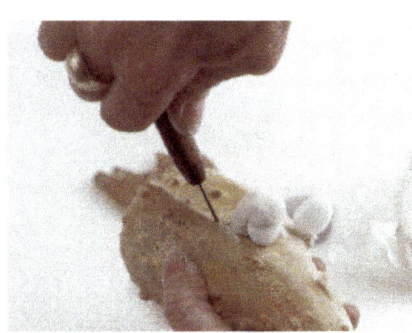

6. Jennifer uses a small awl to make a hole in the gourd for the support pin for the ear.

7. She uses some more air-drying modeling clay to form the moose's small ear around the support pin.

8. If necessary, you can use a small painting brush dipped in water to smooth out the wrinkles in the ear.

See the finished moose brothers on page 180.

Bird, *Jennifer Norpchen*. This is a alternate creature you can make using the same techniques for fashioning the moose.

182 ANIMALS

Frog, *Robert Fox*

Chukar Partridge, *Robert Fox*

Frogs, *Matt Barna*

Birds of a Feather, *Matt Barna*

ANIMALS **183**

Turtle, *David Roseberry*

Bear, *Bill Kupka*

Dog, *Minnie Black. Collection of Ginger Summit.*

Goose, *David Roseberry*

Pyrography

In Peru, carving and pyrography-coloring animals made from gourds has been a tradition for the past fifty years. (Heat engraving or pyrography uses fire [*pyro-*] or heat to draw [*-graphy*] on the gourd's surface.) Their intricate carving, with details of infinitesimal size, has been a tradition in the villages of Cochas Chicas and Huancayo for at least a hundred years. Yet the desire for gourd designs that were quicker to complete and perhaps more appealing to the "modern" taste resulted in the marketing of whole-animal gourds, while still using tried-and-true carving and burning techniques in villages without electricity or telephones.

Traditional Peruvian carved bird, Julio Seguil Rios

PROJECT 28

Rodent

Artist Tito Medina created this *Rodent* that involves pyrography.

1. Tito Medina uses a pencil to indicate the placement of the eyes on a small dipper gourd.

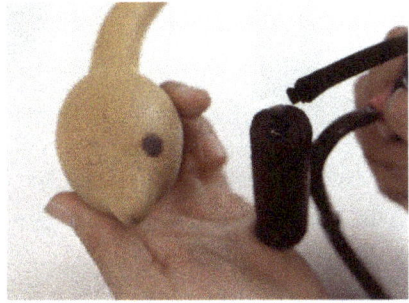

2. With a small homemade torch, he burns in the eye circles.

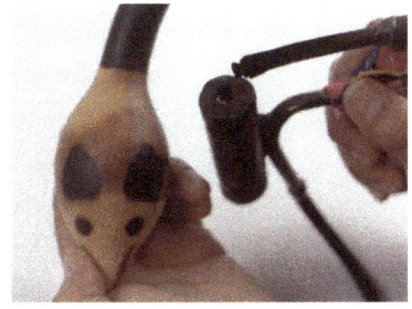

3. After burning the tail and ears, he uses a sweeping motion with the torch to heat the body of the animal and turn the skin a light brown. (Through burning, Tito can achieve at least six distinct color tones from black to very light tan.)

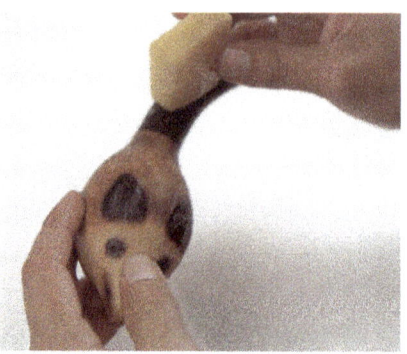 

4. After heating a block of beeswax with the torch, he rubs the softened wax on the gourd.

6. Adding more detail, he uses his burin to carve the white circles around the eyes.

 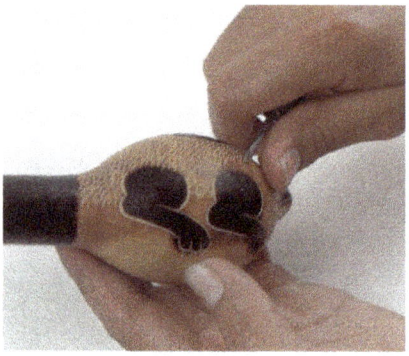

5. He then reheats the wax so that it will be absorbed into the gourd.

7. He carves around the darkened legs to give them distinction and then carves texture into the body.

CHAPTER FIFTEEN
Gallery

Sammy Crawford

Sammy Crawford's earliest memory of gourds was of the dipper that hung by her grandmother's well. Yet as she grew up, she had no idea of the range of their different shapes. After trying to imitate the painting styles of other people, she discovered gourds as a medium for her artwork, and her own original creativity began to flow. "Most of the time, I see a gourd," she says, "and what it is just leaps out at me. They speak to me much more often than I speak to them, and I love that! I seem to enjoy a relationship with my little people. As for embellishments, the gourds themselves seem to know better than I what they need." When completing a new piece, she feels she has taken parts of nature and created something that never existed before.

Bucky, *Sammy Crawford*.
Photo by the artist.

188 GALLERY

Red-Hatter Martha, *Sammy Crawford. Photo by the artist.*

Fast-Food Fanny, *Sammy Crawford. Photo by the artist.*

Oak Leaf Fairy, *Sammy Crawford. Photo by the artist.*

Robert Brady

Artist Robert Brady has been intrigued with gourds. He says, "They are beautiful forms and no two are alike. There is endless variation. I often use found objects in my work. The gourd is an example of a found object. I look at one and imagine what I could make out of it or how I can incorporate it into a larger idea. As with other found objects, my intent is to utilize its qualities or parts of it and transform it so that it takes on yet another life. I allow a conversation with the material, the process, and myself to occur. If I do not over-control, subtleties and changes develop beyond my original concept, which result in a more complex and surprising piece."

Bird #4, *Robert Brady.*
Photo by the artist.

Pat Boyd

Crafter Pat Boyd never considered herself an "artist" until she started making and selling wearable art. Her sister introduced her to gourds as a medium for crafts and made her aware of the tremendous creative potential within all the gourd forms.

She usually begins with an egg gourd that she moves all around the main gourd, which will be the body, trying to decide what it will be doing or expressing. Embellishment comes only after she completes the piece, and what she selects is intended especially for the individual piece.

When she can "take a simple gourd and speak to someone's heart, through figurative gourd art, that's the sacred part," Pat says.

A Sense of Blessing, *Pat Boyd*

Fetchin' II, *Pat Boyd*. Photo by Jim Stephens Studios.

GALLERY **191**

Above, Traveling Elder, *Pat Boyd. Photo by Jim Stephens Studios.*

Left, Primitive Pursuit, *Pat Boyd. Photo by Jim Stephens Studios.*

192 GALLERY

Miracles of Life, *Pat Boyd*. Photo by *Jim Stephens Studios*.

Bag Lady, Carrier of Hope, *Pat Boyd*

Lillian Hopkins

When Lillian Hopkins saw what her friend had made in a gourd-decorating class and the different techniques she had used, Lillian says, "It was like being struck by lightning! All the various techniques and skills I had acquired over the years could be used on gourds! They looked like the perfect medium for me. I was making art dolls from polymer clay at the time, but didn't enjoy sewing the clothing. The bottle gourds I saw looked to me like bodies that just needed heads and limbs, and I could do all kinds of things with the clothes without having to sew."

When creating a doll, Lillian has an image in mind before she begins working on the gourd, and she constantly refers to that image as she goes along. "Usually some parts of the image are not as clear as others," she explains. "For example, I may not know exactly what decoration is supposed to be down the front, but I know what it's supposed to feel like. Usually I use the patterning in the shell of the gourd itself to guide and inspire me, and I also look through design books to help me come up with the right design."

Turquoise and Feather Southwest Spirits, *Lillian Hopkins*

Wind Spirit, *Lillian Hopkins*

194 GALLERY

Tree Spirit, *Lillian Hopkins*

Adinkra Dream Spinner, *Lillian Hopkins*

Little Sleeping Storyteller, *Lillian Hopkins*

GALLERY **195**

Conversation, *Lillian Hopkins*

Carved Diamonds Storyteller, *Lillian Hopkins*

Fetish Pot, *Cass Iverson*

Cass Iverson

As a child growing up in Missouri, Cass Iverson and her brothers and sisters found buffalo gourds along the creek banks and played with them. As an adult, she always enjoyed planting unusual things in the garden, so gourds were a natural choice. She first started working with gourds from her garden. "It was love at first sight," she says. "I handpick the gourds to work with, or maybe I should say they pick me. The gourds and I speak to each other. Mostly they tell me what they want to be, but sometimes I make a suggestion. After working with gourds for over twenty-three years, I must say that they have shaped my life. I am happiest when I am creating something new. Besides, gourds have introduced me to some of the nicest people on the planet."

Fish, *Cass Iverson*

African Drummer, *Cass Iverson*

GALLERY **197**

Monkey, *Cass Iverson*

Happy Buddha, *Cass Iverson*

Kokopelli, *Cass Iverson*

Madonna, *Cass Iverson*

198 GALLERY

Knight, *Cass Iverson*

Warrior, *Cass Iverson*

Dog, *Cass Iverson*

Nancy Miller

Nancy Miller discovered her artistic voice when she began working with gourds. "The magical element that showed me I could 'sing' was the lowly gourd," she says. "What is wonderful is that the gourd and I are on the path together. My work is a true dialogue with my material. We inspire each other. The dialogue begins amidst the grower's pile of gourds. I have no idea what will become of the gourds I am drawn to buy. I am very eclectic in my materials—mostly natural elements that I fondly refer to as 'dried dead things.' I have a roomful of embellishments and a basement full of gourds, so I am always finding things that just don't work for one project and turn out to be perfect for another."

Spirit of the Gourd, *Nancy Miller*

Larry McClelland

Larry McClelland, a tole painter, found a craft magazine with an ad for gourds. "I knew about gourds from family vacations. There would be baskets of dried gourds at farm stands, especially in the fall. I ordered a box of gourds from a farm in Texas in 1994 and started doing crafts with them. My skills developed and I learned of gourd farms closer to home." He went to a gourd festival and soon started doing his own thing, making gourd critters.

He likes gourd competitions because they challenge him, Larry says. "In the last twelve years there has been a major evolution from gourd crafts to really fine gourd art among the gourd community."

When creating a piece, he has a vision of the final image and thinks about the steps he needs to take to complete it. "When I look at a pile of gourds, sometimes individual gourds will look like a sea otter, a quail, or a snail. But so much of what I do is assemblage of gourd components—it's like sculpture. The gourd is the starting point, but not necessarily the finishing point." He works with a variety of applied colors as well as the gourd's natural color.

Dream Kachina, *Larry McClelland*

Green Bug with People Feet, *made from a crown-of-thorns gourd and devil's claws, Larry McClelland*

Winged Warty Whatsit, *Larry McClelland*

Diane Piccola

Artist Diane Piccola found that working with gourds took her talent to another level of creativity. While attending a gourd show in California in 1999, "what joy and excitement came over me," she says, "when I saw the beautiful and creative things the artists were doing. A car full of gourds came home with me, and I developed a passion for their natural and magical beauty.

"When starting a project, I may sketch several ideas, and then I will pick the right pieces. I get so caught up in each doll that I talk to them and they talk back to me with their eyes and smiles. The gourds make me feel happy, connected, and seem to have magical healing properties. Working with them is my form of daily meditation." She believes that if you're true to yourself and your spirit, do what you love and love what you do, what you produce will be ingrained in your soul.

Above, Pecoquette, *Diane Piccola*

Far left, Sierra, *Diane Piccola*

Left, Treasures, *Diane Piccola*

GALLERY **203**

Nature Ali, *Diane Piccola*

Gypsy Spirit, *Diane Piccola*

Dyan Mai Peterson

A self-taught artist, Dyan Mai Peterson has been working with gourds for over ten years, while exploring a wide range of media, styles, and subject matter. She is fascinated by gourds' simple shapes, sizes, and textures as well as their many uses in different cultures through the centuries. By combining found objects, such as rusty wire, nails, twisted vines, and plant material, she tries to stay as true to the natural gourd as possible. "My love of nature and the human figure has led me to create what I call 'contemporary figurative sculpture,'" she says. Dyan grows her own gourds in North Carolina and loves the fact that she can grow her own canvas.

Anna and Asama from the Land of Ainu, *Dyan Mai Peterson. Photo by Tim Barnwell, Asheville, North Carolina.*

Seven Brothers, *Dyan Mai Peterson. Photo by Tim Barnwell, Asheville, North Carolina.*

Opie and Linda O'Brien

Opie and Linda O'Brien share an artistic vision, but on somewhat different paths. Opie is an artist and a musician; Linda is also an artist, primarily using pyrography (heat engraving). Their interests converge in the gourd pieces that they create together. From the beginning, gourds were magical for them, and the gourds seemed to have their own voice that dictated what they would eventually become.

Their dolls and figurative pieces express both whimsy and sacredness. As artists working exclusively with organic, recycled, and found materials, they have discovered that the combination of certain materials produces its own natural embellishment.

The O'Briens often travel to Mexico, and their work is influenced a great deal by pre-Columbian art.

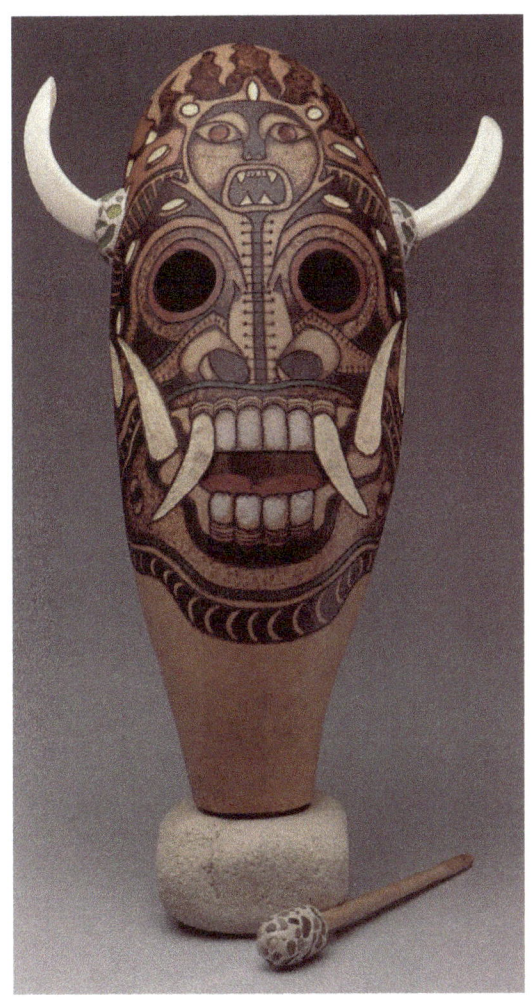

The Nagual, *Opie and Linda O'Brien*. Notches have been carved into the back of the head, so that the instrument can also be played by dragging a stick across the notches to create a rasping sound.

Soulmates, *Opie and Linda O'Brien*

David Roseberry

David Roseberry, when reading books and studying designs of the Southwest, began to incorporate small gourds in his art. "I created potterylike gourds with Native images. As new varieties of gourds crossed my path, new ideas began to emerge and I took a new approach. I began gourd modeling. I spent the next two years finding the right adhesives and body fillers to make the gourd do what I had imagined in my head. I personally select or grow each and every gourd that goes into one of my models. I also prefer dirty over precleaned gourds. More bonding time I guess. I have spent as much as five hours looking for just one gourd to complete a project. Am I crazy?

"The gourd is a very old and wise fruit. Historically speaking, the gourd was a major component of early agriculture everywhere in the world. The use of gourds as portable water vessels and storage jars led the way toward modern pottery in the Southwest and possibly the world. Many early cultures considered the gourd a gift sent from the heavens to make their hard life a little easier, and I guess I do too."

Koshari, *famed clown of the Southwest Pueblos, David Roseberry*

Storyteller, *first crafted in the 1960s among the Pueblos of the Southwest, David Roseberry*

GALLERY **207**

Ranger Holiday, *inspired by an actual ranger stationed at the Navajo National Monument, David Roseberry*

Mountain Giant, *inspired by Robert Mirabal Indian Dance Theater, David Roseberry*

Jill Walker

Former Peace Corps volunteer and frequent traveler Jill Walker encountered gourds many times. "Little did I know that the gourds I observed being used in daily activities and as a basis for folk-art objects would become the focus of my own passion. I had purchased gourd art in Peru and Mexico and gourd bowls in Haiti, but didn't really recognize them for what they were until I became involved with gourd art myself.

"The birth of a doll from its gourd components is particularly soulful. Although I choose the gourds and have a general idea of how I wish to proceed, the spirit of the doll soon begins to emerge and starts to dictate the direction I go. My studio often becomes covered with a wide array of fabrics, leather, beads, and other embellishments as I begin to consider how the doll will be adorned. Not infrequently, even I am surprised at the final result.

"Some of my gourd creations are intended to be playful and whimsical, such as those meant to be used as toys. Gourd dolls as representations of the human form not surprisingly evoke a certain amount of spiritual humanity. I certainly feel their spirituality emerge during the creative process, and I see that those who observe my creations are touched by their spirit as well."

Belled Cat, *Jill Walker*

Ice Man, *Jill Walker*

THE SPIRIT IN THE GOURD 209

Above, Jumping Man, *with wax-resist bobble feet*, Jill Walker

Turtle Woman, *Jill Walker*

Rustic Doll, *with driftwood limbs*, Jill Walker

Marcella Welch

Marcella Welch has been a doll artist for more than twenty-five years, making hundreds of dolls with various media. She first encountered gourds as dippers by wells in Georgia while a child. Later, on a trip to Africa, she saw gourds being used for many different functions. It wasn't until some time after that that she finally found a gourd that inspired her to use them in her doll creations. Now she selects her gourds from her mother's garden in Georgia. "Why I pick one gourd over the other, even though they are similar in shape, is beyond me," she says. "It's almost like they are saying, 'Pick me, pick me, I want to become a beautiful doll.'"

She sculpts the faces and hands to add a dimension that can't be achieved by paint alone. Then she uses dyes and paints for designs, but generally tries to leave much of the natural gourd showing.

Rejoice, *Marcella Welch*

Emerge, *Marcella Welch*

GALLERY 211

Queen Gourd, *Marcella Welch*

Evolving, *Marcella Welch*

Don Weeke

Don Weeke began his career in art as a basket maker, and while collecting willow in a stream bed, noticed some interesting shapes in a nearby field. Since that beginning, he has combined gourds and basketry techniques to create wonderful works of art. The source of his inspiration can come from either the gourd itself or other items that he uses in his work, such as a twig or branch. When working on a large sculptural piece, he first selects the gourd that will be used as a head and then weaves the body of the figure. The embellishments come only after the figure is largely complete. For him, the gourd itself is not sacred; rather, it is the process of creating that is the mysterious force.

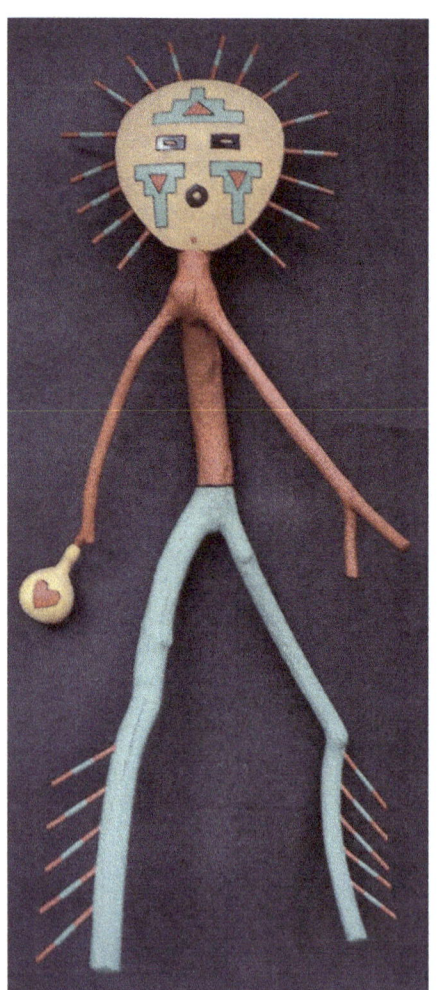

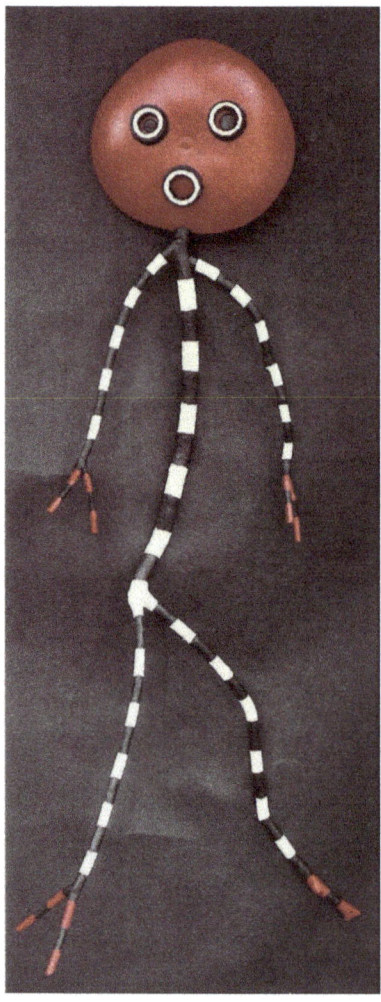

Above, Keeper of the Spirit, *Don Weeke*

Left, Heart Gourd Warrior, *Don Weeke*

Far left, Woodpecker, *Don Weeke*

GALLERY 213

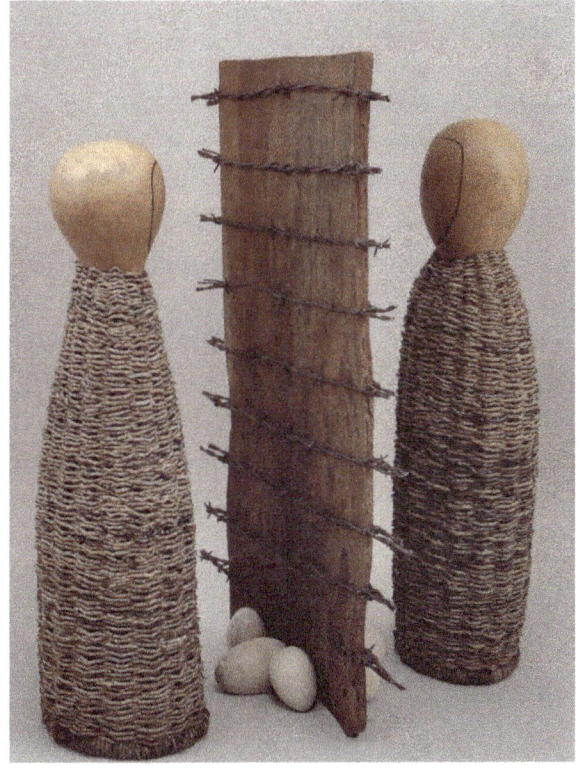

Don't Stop the Conversation, *Don Weeke*

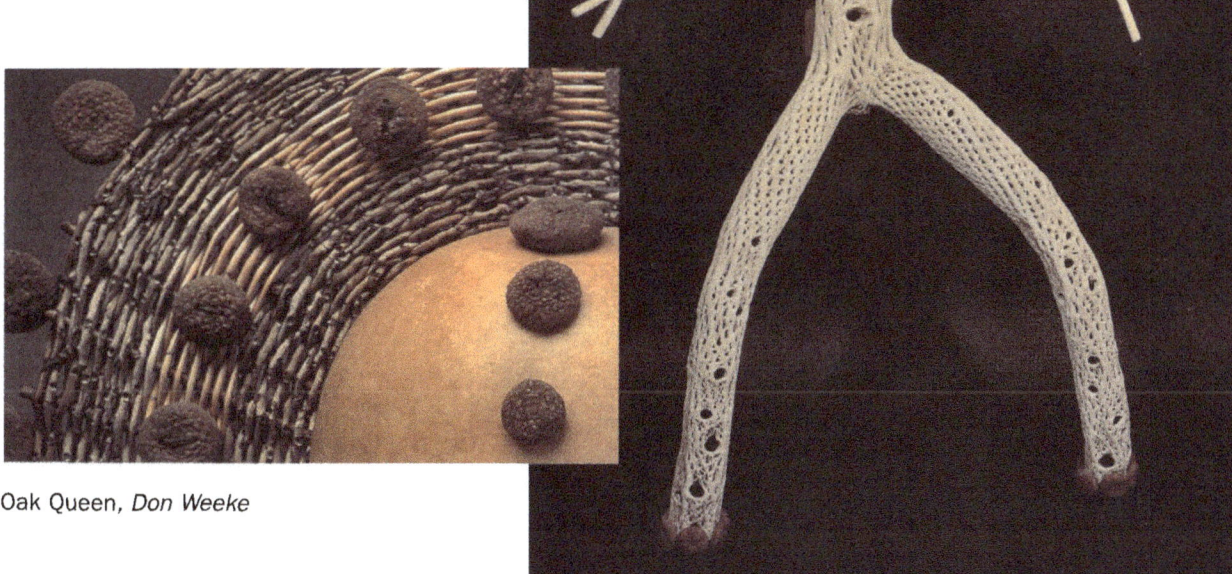

Oak Queen, *Don Weeke*

Lo-Carb Kachina, *Don Weeke*

Angela Briggs

Professionally, Angela Briggs has worked as a graphic artist and a technical artist. Her art experience spans more than forty years, enabling her to incorporate a range of materials, including fiber, clay, wire, wood, and metals, into her work. "Doll-making is much more than it implies," she says. "It is my history. I create altar dolls designed to hold precious keepsakes and other things you can use on an altar or a personal shrine. I release part of my soul and self into my works of art along with knowledge I've collected from ancestral memories. My art expresses feelings of pain, sorrow, hurt, joy, and happiness. With each new piece, I strive to capture and reveal my experience first as a human being and second as an African-American woman."

African doll with open stomach view, Angela Briggs

African doll with grass skirt and straw headband, Angela Briggs

Gourdmaster Sam X

Gourdmaster Sam X first encountered gourds at a local flea market. Before working with gourds, he had never considered himself an artist. "Gourds allowed me to do art I had always visualized but never seen," he says. "In the beginning, the gourds spoke to me, and when they spoke, I listened. Now I select the gourd that projects the image in my mind.

"While creating my sculptures, I can feel the presence of my African ancestors guiding me, teaching me, and showing me the ways of the ancient ones."

He feels a certain sacredness about gourds. "Gourds are sometimes used as a healing medium in the spiritual and medical fields. They are also used in marriage, naming, and dancing ceremonies. The touch, sound, taste, even the smell of a gourd is sacred," Sam X says.

For the Love of You, *Gourdmaster Sam X*

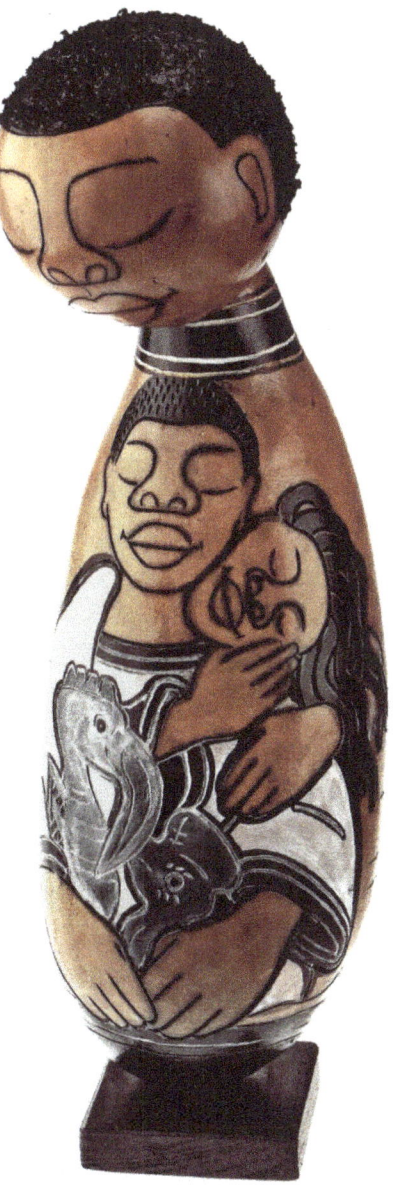

Lovers' Holiday, *Gourdmaster Sam X*

216 GALLERY

Masai Mother and Twins,
Gourdmaster Sam X

The Girls' Party Boat,
Gourdmaster Sam X

Pray for Peace,
Gourdmaster Sam X

GALLERY 217

Love Birds, *Gourdmaster Sam X*

Invoking Spirits, *Gourdmaster Sam X*

Index of Artists and Artwork

Also see General Index beginning on page 221.

Adams, Leigh, 37
  figure from collapsed gourd, 37
  Flower Fairy, 37

Baldonado, Ray
  The Gathering, 119

Barna, Matt
  Birds of a Feather, 182
  Frogs, 182
  Lady of the Lake, 28

Begin, Susan, 48
  Gourdling, 48

Bevans, Nancy, 119
  Statue of Liberty, 119

Bishop, Gerri
  Aunt Mabel at Mardi Gras, 47

Black, Minnie
  Dog, 183
  Dragon, 179

Black, Rebecca
  clown hand puppets, 168

Boyd, Pat, 190–192
  Bag Lady, Carrier of Hope, 192
  Fetchin' II, 190
  Miracles of Life, 192
  Primitive Pursuit, 191
  A Resting Place, 136
  A Sense of Blessing, 190
  Traveling Elder, 191

Brady, Robert
  Bird #4, 189

Briggs, Angela, 214
  African doll with grass skirt and straw headband, 214
  African doll with open stomach, 214

Brunswig, Jennifer
  Old Boyfriend Doll, 8

Buhler, Marilyn, 30
  Serenity, 30

Bunt, Lynne, 84
  Crone, 84
  Gourd Shaman, 84
  Grandmother, 84

Burton, Cathy, 139
  Day of the Dead, #2, 139
  Day of the Dead, #3, 139
  simple wire armature, 67

Cala, Cookie
  Broken Spirits pin, 175
  Fandango pin, 173
  From Within, 109
  Night Out, 110
  three-part twining technique, 110

Colligen, Bill, 23
  fetish pot, 23

Comerford Leah
  Bluebird pendant, 175
  gourd with pyrography engraving, 10
  Tapir pendant, 175

Cooley, Jo, 94
  angel ornament, 176
  Buddha, 33
  Fu Hi, 90
  Maia, 95
  Melody, 94
  Shin Mu, 94

Crawford, Sammy, 187–188
  Bucky, 187
  Fast-Food Fanny, 188
  Oak Leaf Fairy, 188
  Red-Hatter Martha, 188

Dawson, Lynette, 138
  Bounty, (with open shelves), 138
  Japanese stacked dolls, 95
  Message Doll, 138
  stacked-gourd figure, 95

Dial, Kristi, 83
  The Elder, 83
  Joy, 51
  Maiden, 32

Djuhadi, Ratna (Ardee), 137
  Mother and Child, 137

Driussi-Yaber, Mary, 87–88
  dancing Native American in traditional attire, 88
  Mexican Musician, 87
  Native American spirit doll, 87

Duncan, Pat
  Betsy (Crown of Thorns), 70
  The Golfer, 89

Mr. Ugly, 38
Pickle-Puss mold dolls, 36, 39

Easley, Deborah, 29
  La Llorona, 29

Eichwald, Linda
  jointed doll in clothing and scarf, 60

Embry, Sidney
  African *"Voodoo,"* 27

Erhart, Melissa, 54
  Talking with God, 54

Finch, Betty
  gourd figure with sculpted clay face, 80
  marionette with movable joints, 64

Flores, Tia
  Blessings pin, 175
  Medicine Woman pin, 175

Fox, Robert
  Chukar Partridge, 182
  Frog, 182
  Sun Bottle, 121

Gibson, Bonnie, 101
  Counting Coup, 101
  Crow Mother, 100
  Mud Man, 101, 157

Gittings, Geri, 28
  Gourd Maiden, 28

Goshen, Sherry
  Gift Snatcher, 81

Gourdmaster Sam X, 215–217
  For the Love of You, 215
  The Girls' Party Boat, 216
  Invoking Spirits, 217
  Love Birds, 217
  Lover's Holiday, 215
  Masai Mother and Twins, 216
  Pray for Peace, 216

Haddad, Fonda
  African Lady, 137
  Madonna Gourd Lady, 109
  Navaho Weaver, 109

Hall, Lavonne
  figure with clay parts, 89

Hensen, Doris
  Sprout, 139

INDEX OF ARTISTS AND ARTWORKS

Hogan, Heather, 56
   Spirit Doll with Crystals, 50
   Wyvern, 56

Hopkins, Lillian, 193–195
   Adinkra Dream Spinner, 194
   Carved Diamonds Storyteller, 195
   Conversation, 195
   Little Sleeping Storyteller, 194
   Tree Spirit, 194
   Turquoise and Feather Southwest Spirits, 193
   Venus of Willendorf, 11
   Wind Spirit, 193

Huff, Colleen, 80
   Asian Grace Series, 80

Hunter, Gabrielle
   gourd doll with attached arms, 45

Hurley, Gale
   Kouda, Keeper of the Gourds, 106
   She, 106

Irwin, Robert, 44
   stump-like doll, 44

Iverson, Cass, 196–198
   African Drummer, 196
   Dog, 198
   Fetish Pot, 196
   Fish, 196
   French Chef, 26
   Happy Buddha, 197
   Knight, 198
   Kokopelli, 197
   Madonna, 197
   Monkey, 197
   Warrior, 198

Jordan, Sue, 122
   Corn Maiden, 122

Jordan, Suzanne, 55
   Tripod Spirit Doing a Rain Dance, 55

Kinney, Shirley, 49
   And the Beet Goes On, 49

Kirchner, Mimi, 72–73
   Celeste, 73
   Hope, 72
   Jane, 73
   Saide, 73

Kobe, Janis, 33
   Mumso, 33

Kupka, Bill
   Bear, 183

Lewis, Barbara, 107
   Plains Woman, 107
   Pot Woman, 107

Loe, Jennifer
   Rattle, 33

Lomayma, Lyle
   Warrior Mouse rattle, 157

Lovejoy, Julie, 85
   The Crone, 85
   Dances with Gourds, 85
   Tituba's Song, 85

Mangliers, Kris
   African wire doll, 67
   Maiden with Burden Basket, 81

Martinell, Valerie
   Goddess Doll, 7

Matsutsuyu, Emiko
   stick puppet, 160

McClelland, Larry, 200–201
   Dream Kachina, 200
   Gourd Goddess, 11
   Green Bug with People Feet, 200
   Winged Warty Whatsit, 201

McClure, Beth, 52
   Keeper of the Keys, 52
   Madonna, 152
   Shaman, 53

Medina, Tito
   carved-and-burned owl ornament, 176
   carved-and-burned Santa ornament, 176
   Rodent project, 185–186

Miller, Nancy, 199
   Spirit of the Gourd, 199

Moreno, Juanita
   Seminole dolls, 42

Moskowitz, Deborah
   Feather Princess, 76

Mygatt, Connie, 35
   Old Bead Stringer, 35
   The Wise One, 35

Noblitt, Linda
   Gourdy Andy, 66

   Gourdy Guys, 74
   Gourdy Mollie, 74
   Mermaid pin, 174
   Out of My Gourd, 74
   Pansy, 51
   Wire-Hair Doll pins, 174

Norpchen, Jennifer
   Bird, 181
   Moose project, 180–181

O'Brien, Opie and Linda, 205
   The Nagual, 205
   Soulmates, 205

Page, Virginia and Wayne
   gourd cat sculpture, 178

Papner, Carol, 30
   Mini Badger Kachina, 31
   Mini Eagle Kachina, 32

Pedro, Amil, 22
   gourd figure with beads and paint, 22
   stylized gourd figure, 22

Peterson, Dyan Mai, 204
   Anna and Asama from the Land of Ainu, 204
   Baby on the Way, 39
   collection items, 15, 16, 17, 20
   Seven Brothers, 204

Piccola, Diane, 202–203
   Gypsy Spirit, 203
   Nametag necklace, 174
   Nature Ali, 203
   Pecoquette, 202
   Sierra, 202
   Treasures, 202

Potter, Carolyn
   Goddess, 12
   Gwenivere, 82

Rainwater, Lois, 112
   Elephant, 112
   Harry Hedgehog, 112

Richie, Judy
   Kokopelli, 105

Riker, Kathy
   snake-gourd figure with headdress, 105

Rios, Julio Seguil
   traditional Peruvian carved bird, 184

INDEX OF ARTIST AND ARTWORKS

Ritz-Frith, Elizabeth, 30
  Pueblo Sun Gourd Doll, 31

Rivera, Robert
  Kachina, 29
  kachina rattle, 157

Roberts, Betsy, 78–79
  Bird-Watcher, 78
  Blue Goddess, 78
  Leopard Man, 79
  Red Spirits, 79
  Sleeping Princess, 79

Roseberry, David, 206–207
  Goose, 183
  Koshari, 206
  Mahé, 50
  Mountain Giant, 207
  Ranger Holiday, 207
  Storyteller, 206
  Turtle, 183

Rousso, Kathy, 111
  Everywhere (mix of Alaska and Guatemala), 111
  Here (Alaska), 111
  There (Guatemala), 111

Sarianen, Marcia, 102
  Spirit Doll, 102

Saunders, Virginia
  Garden-Elf mold gourd head, 38

Schiller, Dawn
  African gourd doll, 113
  Intuit, 88
  L'oeuf, 75
  Pjs, 50
  Wind, Burst, Fire, 116

Schlender, Nancy, 26
  Intuit, 26
  Sundance, 27

Seeger, Jan
  double marionette, 64

Shamana, Beverly, 172
  Agate pin, 172
  Amulet for the Soul pin, 171
  Doll pin, 173
  Geisha pin, 172
  Prayer Hands, 89

Simmons, Mary, 102–103
  Earth Momma, 102
  Fan Dancer, 103
  Green Bug, 58
  Indian Maiden, 53
  Kente Lion, 53
  Mermaid, 103

Smith, Mary Pat, 120–121
  Santa Claus, 120

Stone, Kemper
  gourd trumpet, 156

Summit, Ginger
  beaded gourd doll, 113
  Beggar God, 86
  collection items, 17, 24, 25, 71, 173, 179
  holiday figures (leprechaun and witch), 47
  Humpty-Dumpty, 152
  Little Bo-Peep and the Little Lost Sheep, 164
  netted matryoshka doll, 148
  Pinocchio, 41
  rain stick, 156
  Troll, 47
  weighted doll, with beads around neck, 152
  weighted doll, with button eyes/cloth/beads, 149

Thomas, CeCe
  cat ornament, 176
  country girl ornament, 176
  nun ornament, 176
  nurse ornament, 176

Thomas, Lelia
  gourd-head doll, 70

Tollenaar, Diana, 104
  snake-gourd spirit figure, 104

Trygstad, Thena, 96
  Tomte, 96
  Wizard Wartsanall, 96

Tsai, Christi, 34
  Let Me See, 34
  Love, 34
  rattle, 155
  Sleeping Angel, 34
  stick puppet, 159
  weighted doll, with painted Mandarin top, 152
  weighted doll, with painted polka-dot blouse, 150

Vanderheite, Jo Ann, 136
  gourd-doll container, 136

Vargas, Fernando
  beaded figure, 21
  spirit figure, 21

Walker, Jill, 208–209
  African soft doll, 72
  Belled Cat, 208
  Corn Kachina necklace, 175
  Cradle Board necklace, 173
  Ice Man, 208
  Jumping Man, 209
  Limber Jill, 62
  Rustic Doll, 209
  Turtle Woman, 209

Weeke, Don, 212–213
  Don't Stop the Conversation, 213
  Heart Gourd Warrior, 212
  Keeper of the Spirit, 212
  Lo-Carb Kachina, 213
  Oak Queen, 213
  Woodpecker, 212

Welch, Marcella, 210–211
  Emerge, 210
  Evolving, 210
  Queen Gourd, 210
  Rejoice, 210

Westhues, Sue
  marionette of multicolored gourd "balls," 65
  pop-up puppet, 162

Widess, Andy
  little gourd dolls, 8

Willner, Ardith, 71
  Running Deer, 71

Wojeck, Mary
  gourd doll with arms and legs, 61

Zhang, Cairi and Gang
  Gourd Jim, 40
  molded-gourd Chinese folk god of longevity, 40
  molded-gourd Santa Claus, 40

General Index

Also find artists and their works in the Artist Index beginning on page 218.

Adams, Leigh, 37
Adinkra Dream Spinner, 194
African Drummer, 196
African history
   dolls, 19–20, 135
   musical instruments, 154, 158
African initiation dolls, 152
African Lady, 137
African "Voodoo," 27
African Weighted Doll project, 153
afterlife assistance, 16, 18, 19
Agate pin, 172
Amulet for the Soul pin, 171
amulets/good-luck symbols, 19, 20
Anatolia, dolls from, 16
ancestors, dolls representing, 16
animals, 178–186
   master of (Minnie Black), 178–179
   Moose project, 180–181
   pyrography and, 184–186
   Rodent project, 185–186
Anna and Asama from the Land of Ainu, 204
arms. *See* limbs (adding)
articulated joints. *See* limbs (adding); limbs projects
Asian Grace Series, 80
Aunt Mabel at Mardi Gras, 47
Autumn Spirit in the Tree project, 127–129

Baby on the Way, 39
Bag Lady, Carrier of Hope, 192
Baldonado, Ray, 119
Barna, Matt, 28, 182
beadwork, 113–117
   Beaded Bottle Gourd project, 115–116
   Beaded Gourd, Using Tar project, 117
   with wax, 145
   ways of using, 113
   Zulu Beaded Doll project, 114
Bear, 183
And the Beet Goes On, 49
Beggar God, 86
Begin, Susan, 48
Belled Cat, 208
Betsy (Crown of Thorns), 70
Bevans, Nancy, 119
Bird, 181
Bird #4, 189
Birds of a Feather, 182

Bird-Watcher, 78
Bishop, Gerri, 47
Black, Minnie, 178–179, 179, 183
Black, Rebecca, 168
Blessings pin, 175
Bluebird pendant, 175
Blue Goddess, 78
Bounty, (with open shelves), 138
Boyd, Pat, 136, 190–192
Brady, Robert, 189
Brazil, doll from, 14
Briggs, Angela, 214
Broken Spirits pin, 175
Brunswig, Jennifer, 8
Bucky, 187
Buddha, 33
Buhler, Marilyn, 30
Bunt, Lynne, 84
Burton, Cathy, 67, 139

Cala, Cookie, 109, 110, 173, 175
carved/cut gourd dolls
   about, 118, 121
   Autumn Spirit in the Tree project, 127–129
   carving dolls, 121–134, 146
   Green Man, 131–134
   Spirit of Spring project, 123–124
   Spirit of Summer project, 125–126
   Spirit of Winter project, 130
   using cut shells, 119–121
Carved Diamonds Storyteller, 195
cavities in dolls, 135–142
Celeste, 73
children, dolls for, 10, 18, 19
Chinese doll history, 19, 86, 150
Chinese molded gourds, 40
Christian icons, 18
Chukar Partridge, 182
clay, 75–89
   faces, sculpting, 80–85
   for limbs/other shapes, 86–89
   molds, 76–77
cleaning gourds, 9
cloth bodies, 70–74
Colligen, Bill, 23
Comerford Leah, 10, 175
Conversation, 195
Cooley, Jo, 33, 90, 94, 95, 176
Corn Kachina necklace, 175
Corn Maiden, 122
Counting Coup, 101
Cradle Board necklace, 173
Crawford, Sammy, 187–188
Crone (Bunt), 84
The Crone (Lovejoy), 85
Crow Mother, 100
cut gourds. *See* carved/cut gourd dolls

Dances with Gourds, 85
Dancing Dan, 62, 63
daruma dolls, 150–151
Dawson, Lynette, 95, 138
Day of the Dead, #2, 139
Day of the Dead, #3, 139
decorations, for home, 176–177
Dial, Kristi, 32, 51, 83
Djuhadi, Ratna (Ardee), 137
Dog, 183, 198
Doll pin, 173
dolls
   as afterlife assistants, 16, 18, 19
   as amulets/good-luck symbols, 19, 20
   definitions/perspectives of, 10–15
   as educational tools, 14–15
   etymology of, 14
   as fertility figures, 19–20, 152
   figures/figurines vs., 14
   hidden treasures in, 135–141
   as magical surrogates, 19
   as playthings, 10, 18, 19
   puppets vs., 14, 159
   religion and. *See* spirits/religious practices
Don't Stop the Conversation, 213
Dragon, 179
Dream Kachina, 200
Driussi-Yaber, Mary, 87–88
Duncan, Pat, 36, 38, 39, 70, 89
Dutch dolls, 62

Earth Momma, 102
Easley, Deborah, 29
education, dolls for, 14–15
Eichwald, Linda, 60
The Elder, 83
Elephant, 112
Embry, Sidney, 27
Emerge, 210
Erhart, Melissa, 54
European doll history, 18–19, 45, 59, 131, 135–136, 142
Everywhere (mix of Alaska and Guatemala), 111
Evolving, 210

face recognition/shaping
   earliest dolls, 16
   engaging, 7, 10
   natural inclination for, 7
faces, clay, 80–85
Fan Dancer, 103
Fandango pin, 173
Fast-Food Fanny, 188
Feather Princess, 76
fertility figures, 19–20, 152
Fetchin' II, 190

fetishes, 18, 20. *See also* spirits/religious practices
Fetish Pot, 196
fiber arts, 108–112
    Beaded Bottle Gourd project, 115–116
    three-part twining, 110
    wrapping/netting/weaving, 108–112
    Zulu Beaded Doll project, 114
figures/figurines, dolls vs., 14
Finch, Betty, 64, 80
finger puppets, 166–167
Fish, 196
Flores, Tia, 175
Flower Fairy, 37
For the Love of You, 215
Fox, Robert, 121, 182
French Chef, 26
Frog (Fox), 182
Frogs (Barna), 182
From Within, 109
Fu Hi, 90

gallery, 187–217
The Gathering, 119
Geisha pin, 172
Gibson, Bonnie, 100, 101, 157
Gift Snatcher, 81
The Girls' Party Boat, 216
Gittings, Geri, 28
Goddess Doll (Martinell), 7
Goddess (Potter), 12
The Golfer, 89
Goose, 183
Goshen, Sherry, 81
Gourd Goddess, 11
Gourd Jim, 40
Gourdling, 48
Gourd Maiden, 28
Gourdmaster Sam X, 215–217
gourds
    face recognition/shaping, 7
    heads of, 66–74
    molded, 36–40
    removing mold from, 9
    whole. *See* whole gourds
Gourd Shaman, 84
Gourdy Andy, 66
Gourdy Guys, 74
Gourdy Mollie, 74
Grandmother, 84
Green Bug, 58
Green Bug with People Feet, 200
Green Man
    origins and symbolism, 131
    project, 132–134
Gwenivere, 82
Gypsy Spirit, 203

Haddad, Fonda, 109, 137
Hall, Lavonne, 89
hand puppets, 168
Happy Buddha, 197
Harry Hedgehog, 112
heads, gourd, 66–74
    about, 66
    cloth bodies and, 70–74
    Jesters project, 68–69
Heart Gourd Warrior, 212
heat engraving (pyrography), 184–186
Hemba/Luba pipe, 17
Hemba/Luba rattle, 19
Hensen, Doris, 139
Here (Alaska), 111
hiding things in dolls, 135–141
historic dolls
    Hemba/Luba pipe, 17
    Hemba/Luba rattle, 19
    Indonesian scarecrow, 17
    Mina Perdida effigy, 13
    Tanzanian medicine gourd doll, 16
    Tanzanian *Nyamwezi* doll, 20
    Venus of Willendorf, 11
    whole gourds, 24–25, 29
history of dolls/spirit figures, 16–21. *See also* spirits/religious practices
    in Africa, 19–20, 135, 152
    in Anatolia, 16
    articulated joints, 59
    basic creative forces and, 16
    for children, 18, 19
    in China, 19, 86, 150
    daruma dolls, 150
    definition of dolls and, 10–15
    in Europe, 18–19, 45, 59, 131, 135–136, 142
    examples. *See* historic dolls
    Green Man origins/symbolism, 131
    hiding things in dolls, 135–136
    jigger dolls, 62
    kachina dolls, 100
    nesting dolls, 142
    overview, 16–18
    prehistoric periods, 10–12, 16–18
    in South America, 21
    wrapping dolls, 108
hobgoblins, 45
Hogan, Heather, 50, 56
Holy Family icons, 18
home decorations, 176–177
Hope, 72
Hopkins, Lillian, 11, 193–195
Huff, Colleen, 80
Humpty-Dumpty, 152
Humpty-Dumpty Puzzle Doll, 169
Hunter, Gabrielle, 45

Hurley, Gale, 106

Ice Man, 208
ill people, dolls representing, 19
Indian Maiden, 53
Indonesian scarecrow, 17
initiation dolls, African, 152
inlay, with inlace resin, 147
instruments, 154–158
    hunter's harp, rattles, and other, 155–158
    spiritual significance, 154
Inuit (Schiller), 88
Inuit (Schlender), 26
Invoking Spirits, 217
Irwin, Robert, 44
Iverson, Cass, 26, 196–198

Jane, 73
Jesters project, 68–69
jewelry and ornaments, 171–177
jewelry (wearable art), 171–175
ornaments, 176–177
jigger dolls, 62
Jordan, Sue, 122
Jordan, Suzanne, 55
Joy, 51
Jumping Man, 209

Kachina, 29
kachina dolls, 100
Keeper of the Keys, 52
Keeper of the Spirit, 212
Kente Lion, 53
Kinney, Shirley, 49
Kirchner, Mimi, 72–73
Kitchen Witch
    lore, 59
    project, 57–58
Knight, 198
Kobe, Janis, 33
kokeshi dolls, 91–93
    about, 91
    project, 92–93
Kokopelli (Iverson), 197
Kokopelli (Richie), 105
Koshari, 206
Kouda, Keeper of the Gourds, 106
Kupka, Bill, 183

Lady of the Lake, 28
La Llorona, 29
legs. *See* limbs (adding)
Leopard Man, 79
Let Me See, 34
Lewis, Barbara, 107
Limber Jack, 62

Limber Jill, 62
limbs (adding), 41–65
    about, 41
    arms and legs, 45–59
    articulated complex joints, 62–63
    articulated joints, 59–61
    of clay, 86–89
    marionettes, 64–65
    stump dolls, 42–44
limbs projects
    Dancing Dan, 63
    Doll with Articulated Joints, 60–61
    Kitchen Witch, 57–58
    Nisse, 46
    Stump Doll, 43–44
Li-T'ieh-Kuai, 86
Little Bo-Peep and the Little Lost Sheep, 164
Little Sleeping Storyteller, 194
Lo-Carb Kachina, 213
Loe, Jennifer, 33
L'oeuf, 75
Lomayma, Lyle, 157
Love, 34
Love Birds, 217
Lovejoy, Julie, 85
Lover's Holiday, 215

Madonna, 197
Madonna I, 52
Madonna Gourd Lady, 109
magical surrogates, 19
Mahé, 50
Maia, 95
Maiden, 32
Maiden with Burden Basket, 81
Mangliers, Kris, 67, 81
marionettes, 64–65
Martinell, Valerie, 7
Masai Mother and Twins, 216
matryoshka dolls
    decorative techniques, 145–148
    history of, 142
    project, 143–148
Matsutsuyu, Emiko, 160
McClelland, Larry, 11, 200–201
McClure, Beth, 52, 53
Medicine Woman pin, 175
Medina, Tito, 176, 185–186
Melody, 94
Mermaid, 103
Mermaid pin, 174
Message Doll, 138
Mexican gourd puppet, 15
Mexican Musician, 87
Miller, Nancy, 199
Mina Perdida effigy, 13

Mini Badger Kachina, 31
Mini Eagle Kachina, 32
Miracles of Life, 192
molded gourds
    naturally collapsed gourds, 36–37
    shaped while growing, 36, 38–40
mold, removing, 9
molds (for shaping)
    clay, 76–77
    gourd, 36–40
Monkey, 197
Moose project, 180–181
Moreno, Juanita, 42
Moskowitz, Deborah, 76
Mother & Children project, 97–99
Mother and Child, 137
Mother Goose project, 141–142
Mountain Giant, 207
Mr. Gourd Head Puzzle Doll, 168, 170
Mr. Ugly, 38
Mud Man, 101, 157
Mumso, 33
musical instruments. *See* instruments
Mygatt, Connie, 35

The Nagual, 205
Nametag necklace, 174
Nature Ali, 203
Navaho Weaver, 109
nesting dolls, 142–148
    decorative techniques, 145–148
    history of, 142
Night Out, 110
Nisse project, 46
Noblitt, Linda, 51, 66, 74, 174
Norpchen, Jennifer, 180–181
Norwegian dolls, 45–46
Norwegian Kitchen Witch, 59

Oak Leaf Fairy, 188
Oak Queen, 213
O'Brien, Opie and Linda, 205
Old Bead Stringer, 35
Old Boyfriend Doll, 8
ornaments, 176–177
Out of My Gourd, 74

Page, Virginia and Wayne, 178
painted gourds
    painting matryoshka dolls, 145
    whole gourds, 26–32
Pansy, 51
Papner, Carol, 30, 31, 32
Pecoquette, 202
Pedro, Amil, 22
Peruvian gourd dolls, 25
Peterson, Dyan Mai, 39, 204

Piccola, Diane, 174, 202–203
Pinocchio, 41
Pjs, 50
Plains Woman, 107
pop-up puppets, 162–163
Potter, Carolyn, 12, 82
Pot Woman, 107
Prayer Hands, 89
Pray for Peace, 216
prehistoric dolls, 10–12
Primitive Pursuit, 191
projects
    African Weighted Doll, 153
    Autumn Spirit in the Tree, 127–129
    Beaded Bottle Gourd, Using Fabric, 115–116
    Beaded Gourd, Using Tar, 117
    Dancing Dan, 63
    Daybreak Pop-Up Puppet, 163
    Doll with Articulated Joints, 60–61
    Fairy Godmother Stick Puppet, 161–162
    Green Man, 132–134
    Humpty-Dumpty Puzzle Doll, 169
    Jesters, 68–69
    Kitchen Witch, 57–58
    Kokeshi Doll, 92–93
    Matryoshka Set, 143–148
    Moose, 180–181
    Mother Goose, 141–142
    Mr. Gourd Head Puzzle Doll, 170
    Night and Day Topsy-Turvy Puppet, 165–166
    Nisse, 46
    Rodent, 185–186
    Spirit of Spring, 123–124
    Spirit of Summer, 125–126
    Spirit of Winter, 130
    Stacked Dolls: Mother & Children, 97–99
    Stump Doll, 43–44
    Three Little Pigs and Little Red Riding Hood Finger Puppets, 167
    Weighted Daruma Doll, 151
    Zulu Beaded Doll, Using Fabric, 114
Pueblo Sun Gourd Doll, 31
puppet projects
    Daybreak Pop-Up Puppet, 163
    Fairy Godmother Stick Puppet, 161–162
    Humpty-Dumpty Puzzle Doll, 169
    Mr. Gourd Head Puzzle Doll, 168, 170
    Night and Day Topsy-Turvy Puppet, 165–166
    Three Little Pigs and Little Red Riding Hood Finger Puppets, 167
puppets, 159–170

dolls vs., 14, 159
finger, 166–167
hand, 168
pop-up, 162–163
puzzle dolls and, 168–170
stick, 160–162
topsy-turvy, 164–166
puzzle dolls, 168–170
pyrography, 184–186

Queen Gourd, 210

Rainwater, Lois, 112
Ranger Holiday, 207
Rattle, 33
rattles and instruments, 154–158
Red-Hatter Martha, 188
Red Spirits, 79
Rejoice, 210
religion. *See* spirits/religious practices
A Resting Place, 136
Richie, Judy, 105
Riker, Kathy, 105
Rios, Julio Seguil, 184
Ritz-Frith, Elizabeth, 30, 31
Rivera, Robert, 29, 157
Roberts, Betsy, 78–79
Rodent project, 185–186
roly-poly dolls. *See* weighted dolls
Roseberry, David, 50, 183, 206–207
Rousso, Kathy, 111
Running Deer, 71
Rustic Doll, 209

Saide, 73
Santa Claus, 120
Sarianen, Marcia, 102
Saunders, Virginia, 38
Scandinavian dolls, 45–46, 59
Schiller, Dawn, 50, 75, 88, 113, 116
Schlender, Nancy, 26, 27
Seeger, Jan, 64
A Sense of Blessing, 190
Serenity, 30
Seven Brothers, 204
Shaman, 53
Shamana, Beverly, 89, 171, 172, 173
She, 106
Shin Mu, 94
Sierra, 202
Simmons, Mary, 53, 58, 102–103
Sleeping Angel, 34
Sleeping Princess, 79
Smith, Mary Pat, 120–121
snake-gourd dolls, 100–107
Soulmates, 205
South American doll history, 21

Spirit Doll, 102
Spirit Doll with Crystals, 50
Spirit of Spring project, 123–124
Spirit of Summer project, 125–126
Spirit of the Gourd, 199
Spirit of Winter project, 130
spirits/religious practices, 12, 16–18
  in Africa, 19–20
  afterlife assistance, 16, 18, 19
  in China, 19
  Christian icons, 18
  doll materials for, 11, 18
  in Europe, 18–19
  fetishes, 18, 20
  Holy Family icons, 18
  human sacrifice and, 16
  kachina dolls, 100
  musical instruments and, 154
  pagan cultures, 18
  prehistoric dolls and, 11–12, 16
  shaman rituals, 18, 20
  surrogate dolls for ill people, 19
  Venus of Willendorf and, 11
Sprout, 139
stacked doll projects
  Kokeshi Doll, 92–93
  Mother & Children, 97–99
stacked dolls, 90–107
  about, 90
  kachina dolls, 100
  kokeshi dolls, 91–93
  snake-gourd dolls, 100–107
Statue of Liberty, 119
stick puppets, 160–162
Stone, Kemper, 156
Storyteller, 206
stump dolls, 42–44
Summit, Ginger, 41, 47, 86, 113, 148, 149, 152, 156, 164
Sun Bottle, 121
Sundance, 27
Swedish dolls, 45

Talking with God, 54
Tanzanian medicine gourd doll, 16
Tanzanian *Nyamwezi* doll, 20
Tapir pendant, 175
There (Guatemala), 111
Thomas, CeCe, 176
Thomas, Lelia, 70
Three Little Pigs and Little Red Riding Hood Finger Puppets, 167
Tituba's Song, 85
Tollenaar, Diana, 104
Tomte, 96
topsy-turvy puppets, 164–166
Traveling Elder, 191

Treasures, 202
treasures, hidden in dolls, 135–141
Tree Spirit, 194
Tripod Spirit Doing a Rain Dance, 55
Troll, 47
Trygstad, Thena, 96
Tsai, Christi, 34, 150, 152, 155, 159
tumbler dolls. *See* weighted dolls
Turkish gourd dolls, 25
Turquoise and Feather Southwest Spirits, 193
Turtle, 183
Turtle Woman, 209
twining, three-part, 110

Vanderheite, Jo Ann, 136
Vargas, Fernando, 21
Venus of Willendorf, 11

Walker, Jill, 62, 72, 173, 175, 208–209
Warrior, 198
Warrior Mouse rattle, 157
wax, beads with, 145
weaving. *See* fiber arts
Weeke, Don, 212–213
Weighted Daruma Doll project, 151
weighted dolls, 149–153
  African initiation dolls, 152
  African Weighted Doll project, 153
  daruma dolls, 150–151
  keeping dolls upright, 149
  Weighted Daruma Doll project, 151
Weighted doll, with button eyes/cloth/beads, 149
Welch, Marcella, 210–211
Westhues, Sue, 65, 162
whole gourds, 24–35
  about, 24
  historic dolls, 24–25, 29
  painted, 26–32
  wood-burned, 33–35
Widess, Andy, 8
Willner, Ardith, 71
Wind, Burst, Fire, 116
Wind Spirit, 193
Winged Warty Whatsit, 201
Wire-Hair Doll pins, 174
The Wise One, 35
Wizard Wartsanall, 96
Wojeck, Mary, 61
Woodpecker, 212
wrapping. *See* fiber arts
Wyvern, 56

Zhang, Cairi and Gang, 40
Zulu Beaded Doll project, 114

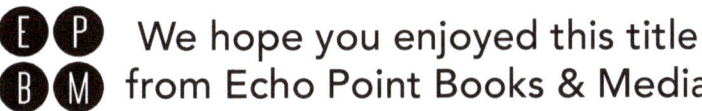 We hope you enjoyed this title from Echo Point Books & Media

---

Before Closing this Book, Two Good Things to Know

Buy Direct & Save

Go to www.echopointbooks.com (click "Our Titles" at top or click "For Echo Point Publishing" in the middle) to see our complete list of titles. We publish books on a wide variety of topics—from spirituality to auto repair.

Buy direct and save 10% at www.echopointbooks.com

DISCOUNT CODE: EPBUYER

Make Literary History and Earn $100 Plus Other Goodies Simply for Your Book Recommendation!

At Echo Point Books & Media we specialize in republishing out-of-print books that are united by one essential ingredient: high quality. Do you know of any great books that are no longer actively published? If so, please let us know. If we end up publishing your recommendation, you'll be adding a wee bit to literary culture and a bunch to our publishing efforts.

Here is how we will thank you:

- A free copy of the new version of your beloved book that includes acknowledgement of your skill as a sharp book scout.
- A free copy of another Echo Point title you like from echopointbooks.com.
- And, oh yes, we'll also send you a check for $100.

Since we publish an eclectic list of titles, we're interested in a wide range of books. So please don't be shy if you have obscure tastes or like books with a practical focus. To get a sense of what kind of books we publish, visit us at www.echopointbooks.com.

If you have a book that you think will work for us, send us an email at editorial@echopointbooks.com

 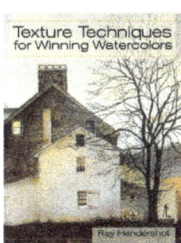   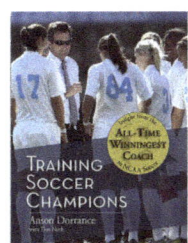

www.ingramcontent.com/pod-product-compliance
Lightning Source LLC
Chambersburg PA
CBHW040928240426
43667CB00026B/2986